Lean Organisations Need FAT People

HOW TO SUCCESSFULLY GROW YOUR HUMAN ASSETS

Bay Jordan

Second Edition

Swanstone Wynot

Lean Organisations Need FAT People
Second Edition
Bay Jordan

Copyright © 2004 Bay Jordan

ZEALISE

Zealise Limited
www.zealise.com

All rights reserved. No part of this publication may be reproduced, stored in a retrieval system or transmitted in any form or by any means, electronic, mechanical, audio, visual or otherwise, without prior written permission of the copyright owner. Nor can it be circulated in any form of binding or cover other than that in which it is published and without similar conditions including this condition being imposed on the subsequent purchaser.

ISBN 0-9768447-4-5

Cover design by Tinracer Design
Original artwork by Bay Jordan and Tim Harries
Layout and typesetting by Robinson Associates

Published by
WYNOT BOOKS
A Division of Swanstone Wynot
Suite 1009, 4607 Cypresswood Drive,
Spring, Texas, 77379, USA
www.swanstonewynot.com

INTRODUCTION

"Man's main task in life is to give birth to himself, to become what he potentially is."
Erich Fromm, American philosopher 1900–1980

Noble sentiment indeed, yet what is a person's potential? It seems to me that potential is the extreme edge of possibility; the point of attainment that remains perpetually just out of reach. Striving to fulfil potential is like trying to grasp the end of the rainbow. Every effort, whilst improving capability, simply increases the scope of what may be. Does that mean that we should never aspire to fulfil our potential? Hardly! Progress is the law of life and a fulfilled life is one of continuous achievement, in which every activity opens the door to something new and leads to new possibilities. Since opportunity almost invariably results from achievement, this means that every opportunity taken is effectively a step towards enhancing potential!

Oprah Winfrey put it as well as anybody when she said:

"My philosophy is that you are not only responsible for your life, but doing the best at this moment puts you in the best place for the next moment."

This is considerably more reasonable and practical. It recognises that potential and perfection are practically synonymous and, since we all know how hard it is to achieve perfection, offers a subtle shift of expectation that is considerably less demanding by acknowledging the fine line between doing one's best (absolute!) and doing one's best "at this moment." If we take an athlete as an example, one's best would entail a personal record – a personal best – every time they compete, while the alternative recognises that there are other factors that come into play and affect the ultimate outcome.

This is an important concept when it comes to measuring personal performance and productivity, because so much is determined by expectation.

I once heard that a steam engine (an external combustion engine) operates at only 10% of its potential capacity and that a steam train could, theoretically, travel in excess of 1000 miles per hour if it had the capability to stay on the tracks at that speed. It would also blow up if the engine reached such optimum performance! So while there is such a phenomenal potential, both actual performance and expectation are considerably lower.

That is probably why steam engines are no longer as widespread as they once were and have been replaced by other forms of engines. So how much nearer perfection are we? Well, my sources of information tell me that the internal combustion engine that powers most petrol driven cars has a coefficient of efficiency of around 0.15 and even for diesel engines it only improves to around 0.20. So while I find the performance of my turbo diesel quite amazing compared to what I was previously accustomed to, it appears that there is definitely scope for considerable improvement!

Before anyone thinks that this is an attack on mechanical engineering or the automotive industry, I hasten to point out that the human body apparently only operates at something in the region of 0.30 or 30% efficiency. If Mother Nature does such a poor job, maybe this isn't so bad and it is unreasonable to expect mankind to do better. So what's my point? Simply that it is to physical science's credit that they even have an idea of how inefficient things are. Management science lacks any kind of comparative yardstick.

An organisation is, by definition, a collection of people assembled to work together to achieve an agreed objective. While this may include overseeing the use of non-human resources, the ultimate concept is no different from that of a machine or organism, where the constituent components all work together to a specified end. Yet we never really pause to measure how effective this body really is. Think about it for a moment. What is the collective intellectual capacity in any organisation and how much of that capacity do we use? "For 25 years you've paid for my hands when you could have had my brain as well – for nothing." This statement by an employee quoted by Jack Welch in his biography encapsulates the point precisely. It points to the unconscious heritage of past times when workers were collectively referred to as "hands" and shows how little we have actually travelled in recognising the human being behind the worker. The following diagram illustrates the wastage graphically, with the centre circle depicting the energy utilised and the outer circle the unproductive resource.

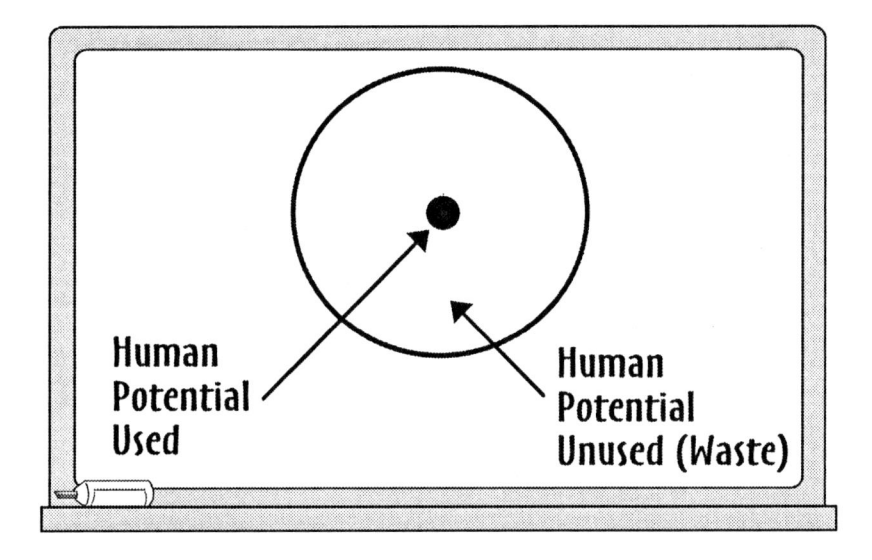

Human Potential Used / **Human Potential Unused (Waste)**

It is perhaps one of the great ironies of the industrial age that countless managers charged with maximising productivity spent their entire working lives seeking to coax additional profits out of businesses and their operations without ever recognising this. Even today, when it is even more imperative to ensure that we do not misuse, and therefore by definition abuse, our human resources, this concept remains barely recognised.

Wastage on this scale makes it inevitable that an organisation will acquire more resources than it actually needs to achieve its ends, compounding the wastage and creating a double whammy for the organisation.

Lean organisations are an attempt to address this waste. Yet all too often they are driven by the need to improve efficiency and cut costs and are driven from the top down, completely oblivious of the fundamental issues that are key to success.

I JUST LOVE THESE COST CUTTING INITIATIVES, DON'T YOU?

This book is an attempt to close that gap and improve organisational effectiveness by acknowledging that it is the people who determine the effectiveness of an organisation and its ultimate success or failure. Thus it looks at organisational energy and what powers it, and identifies ways in which this can be boosted to make the human resources the organisational assets that they truly are, or should be, and thereby underpinning their treatment and valuation.

It illustrates the fact that "leanness" will never be fully achieved through "lean" thinking or the kind of specialisation inherent in mass production methods. Rather it reveals the "paradox" that successful lean organisations require "FAT" employees – people who have the ability to see the big picture and apply their skills outside of the field in which they learned them and which they might traditionally have been expected to. Such people can adapt themselves and their abilities in a wide range of situations and can focus on the team objective rather than their personal advancement.

*"It is the nature of man to rise to greatness if **greatness is expected** of him."* (John Steinbeck, American writer, 1902–1968).[1] The same is true of organisations, but in order to really achieve greatness, they have to create an organisational energy that is rooted in the individual employee and synergised in effective teamwork. Thus they need great people, or, as I prefer to call them, FAT people.

Join me as I explain what I mean by this and explore ideas as to how we can move the boundaries of organisational development to create an environment that stimulates the people who work there, thus allowing them to pursue their own potential and start on the road to greatness.

---

[1] Steinbeck here uses the term "man" in its generic sense to depict Homo sapiens and thus describe both the male and female members of the human race. This may no longer be politically correct but it is both logical and convenient and – with apologies to feminists who may be offended – I will continue to use it in the same vein.

CONTENTS

		Page
1.	Finding FAT people	1
2.	Beyond Maslow	5
3.	Beyond Motivation	15
4.	Beyond Energy	27
5.	'A' is for Awareness and Alignment	41
6.	'A' is also for Assets	53
7.	Time to "'T' on"	73
8.	Beyond Employment	113
9.	Conclusion	127

CHAPTER 1

FINDING FAT PEOPLE

While researchers keep reporting on the increasing size of human beings and their body-fat ratios, hopefully you will have realised that when I say lean companies need FAT people I do not mean that literally. This is not a one-man campaign to put Weight Watchers and the rest of the diet industry out of business! Rather, as already indicated, the image is intended to convey the idea of fuller jobs with greater responsibility and people with the capability to do them justice.

One of the fundamental shifts in working patterns that has resulted from the Information Revolution has been the devolution of power. The speed of transaction and the resultant intensification of competition have eroded the feasibility of traditional hierarchical (top-down) management, as well as the manager's role as the decision maker. Immediacy necessitates on-the-spot decisions and consequently the whole organisational dynamic has changed, evidenced by the removal of layers of management in large organisations and the proliferation of "flatter organisations".

For many this has simply been a cost-cutting exercise to keep pace with the competition. The more progressive companies, however, have been better attuned with the fundamental nature of the shifts and recognised the paradox that has increased the consequences of errors and thus the risk of failure. Hence they have attempted to create more knowledge-based "learning organisations" which, when combined with flatter organisations, has resulted in the term "Lean Organisation" entering the lexicons. Yet all too often this has been driven by efforts to use technology to replace people, and the failure of IT investment to deliver the returns forecast is indicative of a top-down effort which has failed to recognise the shifting paradigm.

Organisational effectiveness is ultimately dependent on teamwork. This means that organisational teamwork is now the essential ingredient for organisational success. There is no place for autocracy in building teamwork, which makes the traditional top-down management style that has dominated Western industry redundant. Until this is recognised and organisations start changing, they will find themselves increasingly lagging behind those in which the benefits of teamwork are recognised and exploited.

Toyota is the archetypical example of this, pioneering "lean production" so successfully that it is now the world's number two auto-manufacturer. It has achieved this despite the efforts of the competition to learn from them and adopt many of the same practices. The failure of the Western auto-manufacturers to achieve the same levels of efficiency is not the result of not understanding the details, but rather of not recognising this fundamental principle. When they have assessed the model they have tended to consider it as being "Japanese" and thus part of their culture. Consequently, they failed to recognise both:

1. The cultural shift that had taken place in Toyota.
2. The need to replicate that culture shift in their own organisations.

I will explore this issue in more depth later, but I am totally satisfied that, whatever the fundamental cultural differences, the Toyota model could be used to greater effect in the West than it has been.

For starters, from my limited knowledge of Japanese history, I would say that the Japanese culture at the end of the war was probably no less autocratic, and possibly more so, than Western culture. One has only to think of the Japanese kamikaze pilots to illustrate that point. There was no Western equivalent!

My confidence, however, is cemented in the beginnings of the Toyota programme after the end of the war, for in the late 1940s the company found itself in a slump and laid off a quarter of its workers.[1]

---

[1] The details of this settlement are outlined in "The Machine That Changed The World" by James P Womack, Daniel T Jones and Daniel Roos, published by Harper Perennial in 1991.

The newly empowered trade unions immediately led a revolt and occupied the factory. After protracted negotiations, a compromise was finally reached whereby the layoffs were allowed to stand, but in exchange the remaining staff members were guaranteed:

- Jobs for life.
- Pay graded by seniority rather than job functions and tied to company profitability through bonus payments.

That is why I am convinced that culture is largely irrelevant. The management reaction in this situation was actually not dissimilar to what it would have been in any Western company. The big difference, though, is the fact that management was forced to re-think the way in which it treated its workers. After all, if they were compelled to pay a high price for them and were powerless to remove them, they damn well had to make sure they made better use of them.

That is the seed – the very essence – of lean production, and those are the principles upon which my case for "FAT" workers is based.

You see, by FAT, I mean **F**ully **A**ligned **T**eam-workers, and to develop fully aligned team-workers entails creating FAT employees.

FAT employees are:

- **F**ulfilled
- **A**ware
- **T**endentious (always ready to promote the cause)

Therefore, a successful lean organisation really does have a need for FAT people, and I will now explain why these qualities are essential and provide some ideas as to how to develop and stimulate them.

It is not just enough to have "fat-cat" executives!

CHAPTER 2

BEYOND MASLOW
"Give us an 'F'!"

Even if the precise details cannot be remembered, most adults have heard of "Maslow's Hierarchy." Since it was published in 1943, Abraham Maslow's "Hierarchy of Needs" has been an essential element of psychological teaching and humanist management thinking. This is because there is no escaping the basic truth that lies behind it. Humans have a number of basic needs which can be categorised and ranked. Over the years there has been considerable academic analysis of the original proposition, which has been embellished every time additional classifications of need have been identified. Thus, while the original model identified only five basic needs, this number has subsequently increased, and currently stands at eight.

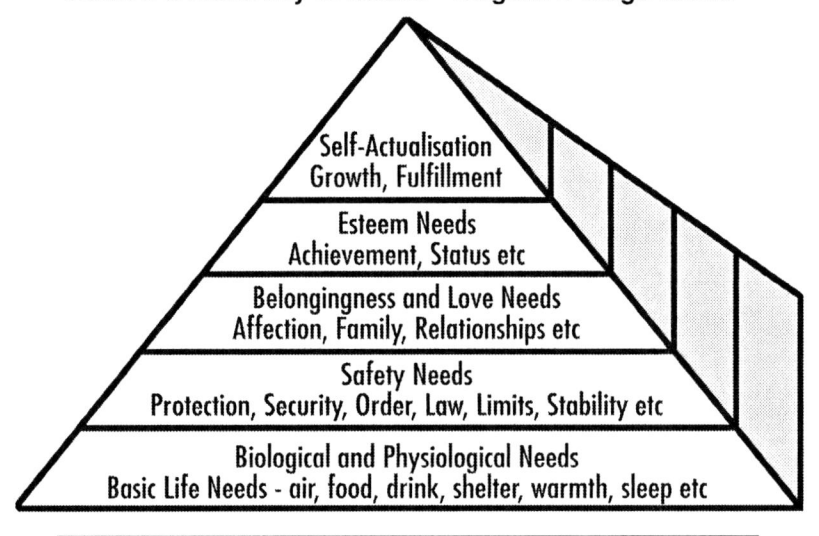

Maslow's Hierarchy of Needs – Original 5-stage model [1]

- Self-Actualisation
  Growth, Fulfillment
- Esteem Needs
  Achievement, Status etc
- Belongingness and Love Needs
  Affection, Family, Relationships etc
- Safety Needs
  Protection, Security, Order, Law, Limits, Stability etc
- Biological and Physiological Needs
  Basic Life Needs - air, food, drink, shelter, warmth, sleep etc

---

[1] These diagrams are largely based on material created by Alan Chapman Consultancy and copyrighted to www.businessballs.com and my debt to them is gratefully acknowledged.

In the 1970s, two additional needs were identified, resulting in the following broader hierarchy.

Maslow's Hierarchy of Needs – 1970s 7-stage model

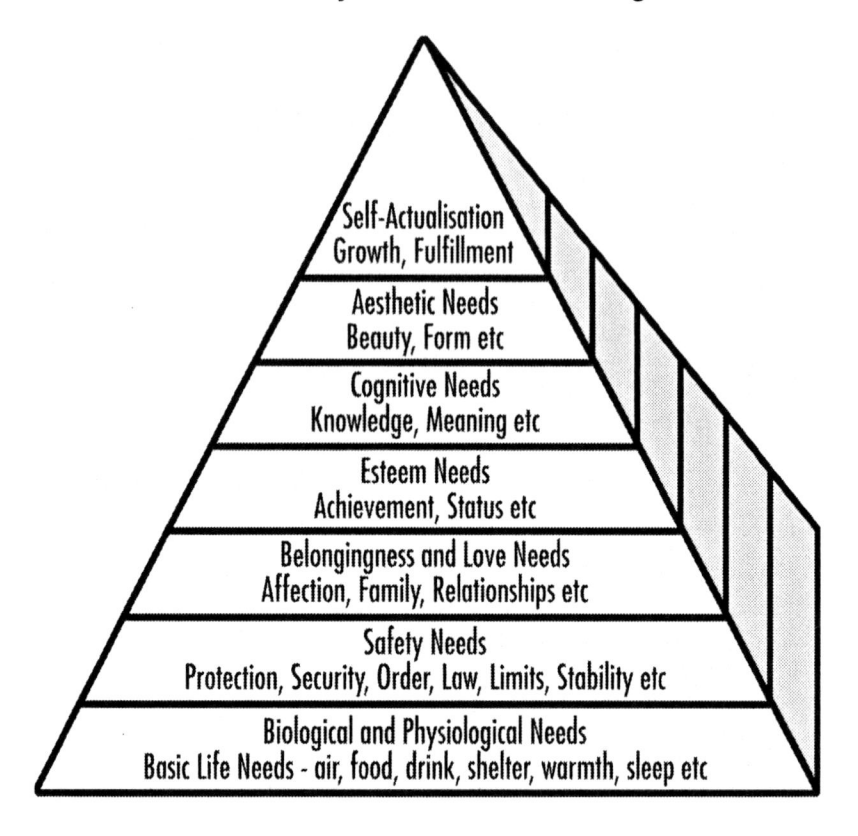

- Self-Actualisation
  Growth, Fulfillment
- Aesthetic Needs
  Beauty, Form etc
- Cognitive Needs
  Knowledge, Meaning etc
- Esteem Needs
  Achievement, Status etc
- Belongingness and Love Needs
  Affection, Family, Relationships etc
- Safety Needs
  Protection, Security, Order, Law, Limits, Stability etc
- Biological and Physiological Needs
  Basic Life Needs - air, food, drink, shelter, warmth, sleep etc

At its most elemental, all that Maslow's Hierarchy does is identify human needs and attempt to rank them in order of priority.

While the completeness and weight assigned to each may be of great importance to psychologists and others attempting to understand the rationale behind human behaviour, the value of such analysis may be disproportionate to the time spent doing so.

In the 1990s, the model was modified further to add yet another hierarchical layer.

Maslow's Hierarchy of Needs – 1990s 8-stage model

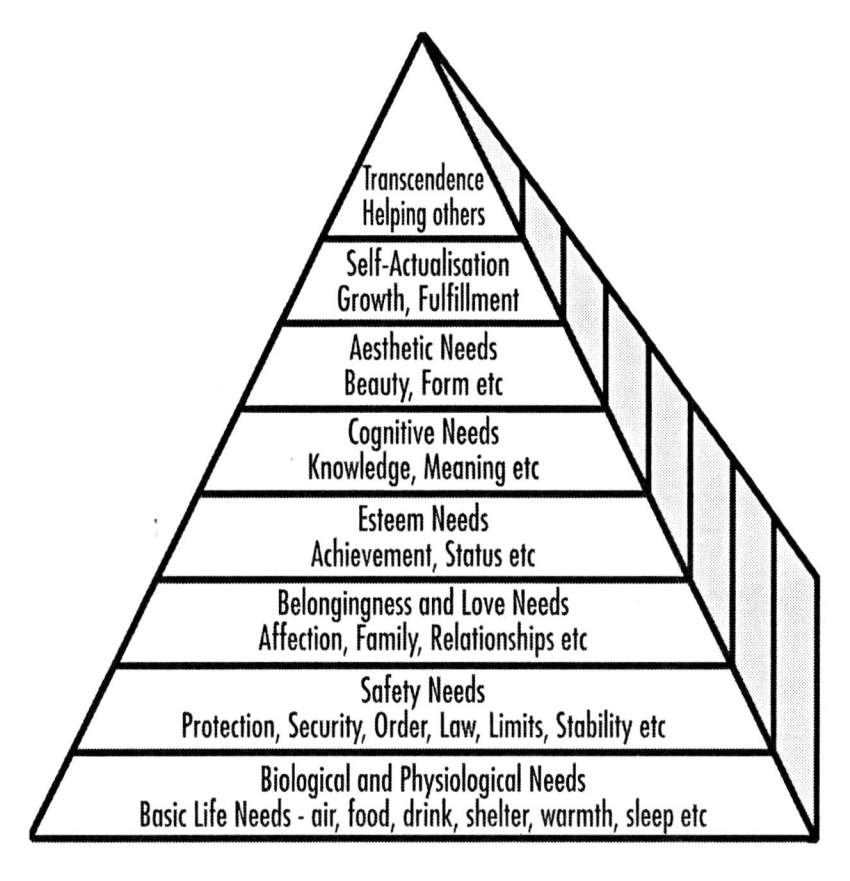

- Transcendence – Helping others
- Self-Actualisation – Growth, Fulfillment
- Aesthetic Needs – Beauty, Form etc
- Cognitive Needs – Knowledge, Meaning etc
- Esteem Needs – Achievement, Status etc
- Belongingness and Love Needs – Affection, Family, Relationships etc
- Safety Needs – Protection, Security, Order, Law, Limits, Stability etc
- Biological and Physiological Needs – Basic Life Needs - air, food, drink, shelter, warmth, sleep etc

Without in any way impugning the validity of such academic thinking, I prefer to take a more simplistic approach. As far as I am concerned, there are only two primary forces that shape human behaviour – desire and demand – with the major differentiation here being that, whereas one is driven by internal forces within the individual, the other is driven by external forces.

However, each of these primary forces can in turn be broken down into different sub-elements.

DESIRE

This is the area where Maslow's Hierarchy becomes relevant, but can nevertheless be simplified into three more fundamental roots:

- Necessity
- Appetite
- Devotion

The terms are my own and are unavoidably limited and by no means definitive, but they are simply used to illustrate a concept. It might perhaps be more scientific to categorise these three elements as primarily biological, physiological and psychological respectively. Irrespective of how one chooses to label them, one encounters the perennial problem of categorisation – definition of both the terms and the boundaries between them. To attempt to do so here would be counter-productive. The key here is not the categories themselves or the boundaries between them, or even the intrinsic characteristic of each, but rather the factors that differentiate them.

As I see it, there are quite simply two such factors:

- Urgency – the time frame in which the desire has to be sated.
- Duration – the period over which the desire impels the activity.

Looked at in this light, the relationship can be depicted in the following table. While this is obviously a rather sweeping generalisation, it nevertheless encapsulates enough fundamental fact to provide pointers for governing behaviour, not least the fact that the only long-lasting behaviour pattern is derived from what I have called "devotion" and is therefore internally (psychologically) driven.

	Urgency	*Duration*
Necessity	Driven by circumstance, usually very urgent or otherwise only urgent when become aware of as a deprivation	Usually short-lived; once the need is sated, the activity either becomes sub-conscious or insignificant
Appetite	May or may not be urgent; not critical if delayed	May be cyclical, but does not normally endure beyond satiation
Devotion	Generally not urgent at all	Usually long-lasting; persists beyond the period when others might have given up

DEMAND

Looking at demand-driven activity in the same way, two primary drivers can be identified.

Stick or Carrot

This time, fortunately, it is not incumbent on me to identify the terms, as these differences are widely accepted and do not need further explanation. However, the relationship between the two can be looked at in the same way.

COMPARING DESIRE AND DEMAND AS FACTORS GOVERNING BEHAVIOUR

This assessment began with the statement that desire was internally driven while demand was externally driven. From an organisational perspective this is an important distinction, because it is a natural progression to say the internal forces are the personal factors affecting behaviour while the demand factors are the group or organisational equivalent.

Desire = Personal Stimulation (Internal)

Demand = External Stimulation (Group/Organisation)

Yet, the analysis reveals remarkable similarities between desire-induced activity and demand-induced activity. Comparing the outcomes at the broadest level, effectively shows:

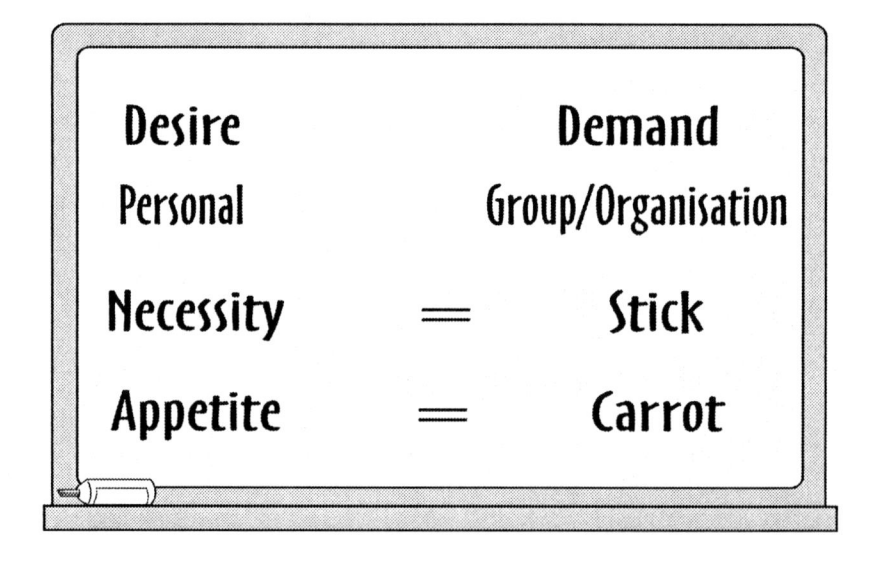

Desire		Demand
Personal		Group/Organisation
Necessity	=	Stick
Appetite	=	Carrot

Since both the stick and the carrot are exclusively external stimuli, the mathematical logic of this equation means that necessity and appetite are also externally stimulated activity drivers. As another term for an external stimulus is an "incentive", this has major implications for shaping organisational behaviour because, as we saw earlier, neither necessity nor appetite are particularly long lasting. Thus incentives, whether positive or negative, will not deliver any long-term benefits, regardless of whether they are desire driven or demand driven.

This is hardly surprising for it is simply a logical extension of the basic economic law of diminishing returns, which identifies that there is less satisfaction for each marginal unit consumed.

However, you will hopefully not have forgotten that there were three elements of desire: necessity, appetite and what I, for want of anything more appropriate, called devotion. We will look at devotion in more depth later, but I see it as that quality which keeps us going, which inspires effort when everything else is conspiring against it.

You will recall that devotion was:

- Innate; dependent on the individuality of the person.

- The only element that had a long-term effect on activity. It is this that provides the clue as to how to proceed further.

The next chart summarises the three fundamental reasons for undertaking activity that I described, and identifies the fact that there is no organisational equivalent of devotion.

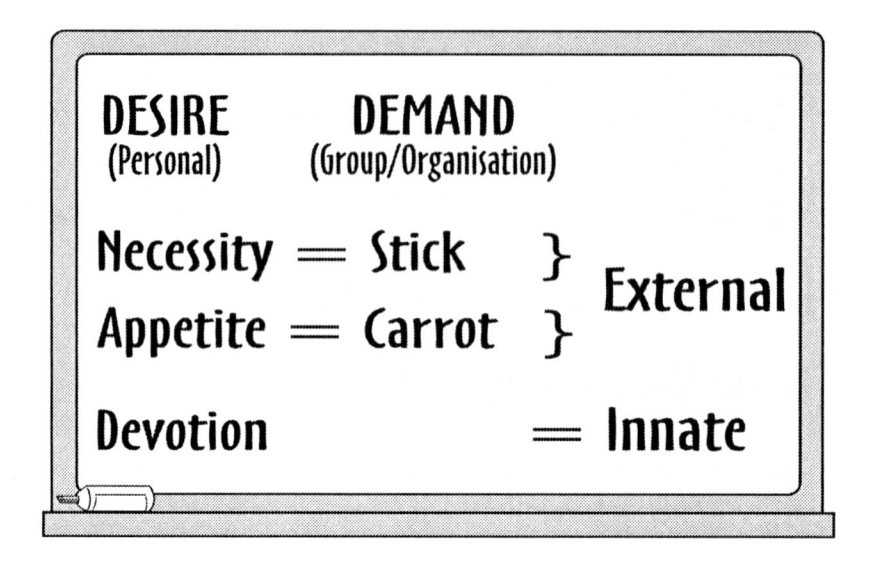

```
DESIRE           DEMAND
(Personal)       (Group/Organisation)

Necessity   =   Stick      }
                           }  External
Appetite    =   Carrot     }

Devotion                   =   Innate
```

It is the space in the demand column that highlights the missing link of organisational behavioural theory. We need to fill the void.

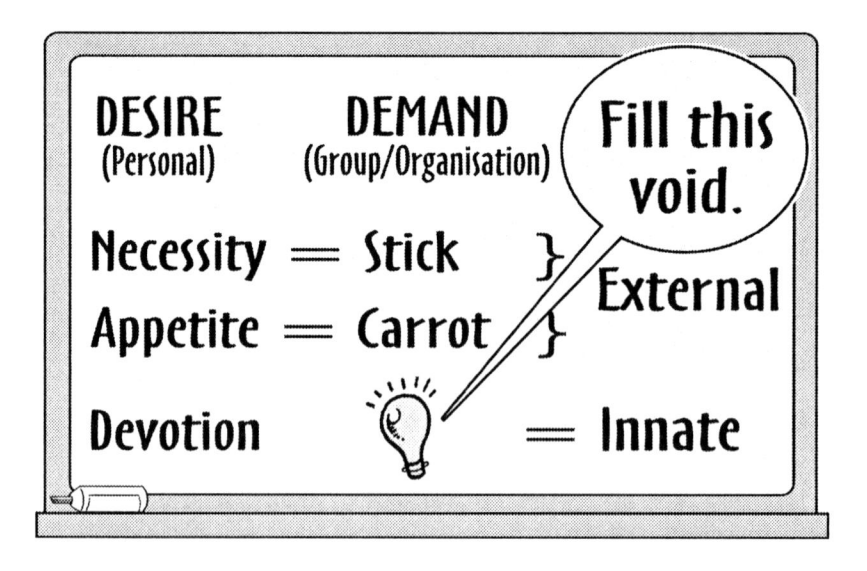

```
DESIRE           DEMAND              ( Fill this
(Personal)       (Group/Organisation)    void. )

Necessity   =   Stick      }
                           }  External
Appetite    =   Carrot     }

Devotion          💡       =   Innate
```

Actually, it is just a case of combining the two, and the challenge is clearly for the organisation to spark that something in the individual that causes them to motivate themselves.

This could be where Maslow's Hierarchy comes in because, since it identifies every human need, it must surely provide some pointers to help the organisation to discover an appropriate tool for this. Yet it seems to be of limited value as an organisational behaviour tool because:

1. Needs have a place in time and circumstance that cannot be circumscribed.

2. While it identifies and ranks human needs, it neither weights them nor provides any means of identifying the point at which they become critical.

3. Every individual is different, and thus the needs and the power to influence behaviour will vary from person to person, as well as in their timing. It would therefore appear unreasonable to expect more precision.

Yet, if Maslow's Hierarchy is complete, as it seems to be, then it must be valid and contain some pointers. For me, the key lies in its completeness, and that is the crucial factor indicating as it does that ultimate personal happiness can only be achieved when all the needs are met – when a person reaches the apex of the pyramid. In other words, a person's happiness is inversely proportional to their level on the pyramid, and until we have reached the point where we are addressing all the identified needs we are never truly happy.

Consequently, to create the spark that will stimulate employees to the point where they motivate themselves, organisations are going to have to move beyond the concepts of traditional "job satisfaction" and work with their people to help them achieve personal fulfilment. This will entail a change in the way organisations look at people that is at least as revolutionary as the one made by Toyota in the 1940s. If this is to be done, it necessitates taking a whole new look at motivation.

Confucius said: *"The superior man is distressed by the limitations of his ability; he is not distressed by the fact that men do not recognise the ability he has."*

I don't know how true the latter part of the statement is in the modern world, but the superior person will certainly not stick around in an environment where there is no opportunity to extend their abilities, while conversely a lesser person just may, whilst not fully using those abilities they do possess.

Which would you rather work with?

CHAPTER 3

BEYOND MOTIVATION

"Were there none who were discontented with what they have, the world would never reach anything better."
Florence Nightingale, 1820-1910

It is hardly new to say that incentives have a limited shelf life and little long-term benefit. There is no obvious reason why the basic economic law of diminishing returns should not apply to incentives as much as it does to everything else. Yet little seems to be done either:

1. To assess just how effective incentives really are.
2. To try to find more effective ways of encouraging greater productivity from employees.

Clearly, to move beyond incentives it is necessary to find some way of creating an "internal stimulus" – something that is innate to the individual. But is this really possible?

MORE THAN SELF-MOTIVATION

"Internal stimulation" is a misnomer for something that I cannot find a better phrase to express. We have already seen that stimuli do not have a lasting effect and thus it hardly makes sense, having pooh-poohed the concept, to start promoting self-generated stimuli as a universal panacea. Apart from anything else, even as individuals we are not consistent!

We all have good days – where nothing seems to stop us and everything just comes together – and bad days where everything that could go wrong seems to do so. There are days when we are energised and unstoppable and days when we are lethargic and "unstartable", where the alarm clock is an absolute drag and just getting out of bed deserves a Victoria Cross! If we are fortunate, the former outnumber the latter by some considerable margin!

But what I am talking about here is the force that keeps us going during those bad days. The times when we soldier on against all the odds and "do what we have to do." What is it that motivates us to do so?

There may be any number of reasons:

- A sense of duty.
- A feeling of not wanting to let the team down.
- The knowledge that there are people depending on you.
- Knowing that if you don't get on, it will just be waiting for you tomorrow.
- Fear of the consequences if you don't.
- Anticipation of the reward when it is done, etc.

Some of these may be internal and some, like the last two, may be external (positive or negative) stimuli. And while they may work sometimes, they will not last indefinitely and sooner or later a "to hell with it!" point is reached. But the risk of anybody being allowed to get close to that point should be guarded against in any commercial or competitive organisation.

FOR THE SHEER PLEASURE OF IT

However, there is often more to it than that. What makes people run marathons? Or play golf regardless of the weather? What is it that inspires effort when everything else is conspiring against it?

Whatever it is, it is more than just self-motivation and it is this quality that we are seeking to identify, find and tap into.

Self-motivation alone is generally not enough to meet and overcome challenges. This requires some kind of coaxing and more than just convincing oneself that "there is no gain without pain!" This is tantamount to self-stimulation and is subject to the same shortcomings as external stimuli. It might work once or twice, but not indefinitely.

Whatever it is that inspires such behaviour, it is often difficult, even for those who experience it, to explain to others. Ultimately it is just something that "makes them feel good". And that is the pod that envelops the answer.

ENJOYMENT IS THE KEY TO DEVOTION

The magic ingredient is joy. It is a love of running that keeps someone running marathon after marathon – the sheer joy of the challenge, the sense of achievement, whatever the result. That is the quality we need to bring to our workplace. So what we need is to create more joy in our working environment.

JOY AND FUN ARE NOT NECESSARILY THE SAME THING

I have always been slightly irritated by organisations that claim to be "a fun place to work". For some reason this statement seems prescriptive and I have visions of managers standing over staff saying, "You vill have fun, ja!" A small part of this reaction may just be the residue of indoctrination and a resultant ingrained puritanism that work is serious and therefore cannot be fun!

However, even when I have challenged the idiocy of that attitude, I have not been able to surmount the sense of disapproval. It only recently dawned on me that this is because I consider "fun" to be the wrong word and "enjoyable" to be the more appropriate term.

Perhaps this is just semantic hair splitting on my part, but for me "fun" conveys a sense of levity that is not what most organisations aspire to.

Enjoyment in no way precludes having fun, but is much more inclusive of many different things, and thus seems so much more democratic!

IS A UNIVERSAL SOLUTION POSSIBLE?

Regardless of the terminology used, it would appear that "work is fun" attitudes are at least a step in the right direction towards making work more enjoyable. However, is this a realistic goal? After all, the only certainty is that everyone is different; as individuals, not only do our responses vary according to our moods, but we all enjoy different things.

So is it possible to have a system that allows everyone to "do their own thing"?

Many other recent initiatives appear to have recognised the individual and the need to manage differently. Amongst them are:

- Performance Related Pay
- "Cafeteria" Pay and Benefit Packages
- Job Sharing
- Work from Home
- "Work-Life Balance"

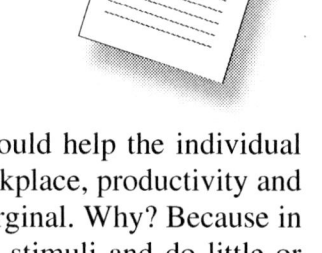

While such efforts undoubtedly should help the individual and bring more enjoyment into the workplace, productivity and performance improvements remain marginal. Why? Because in the majority of cases they still remain stimuli and do little or nothing to encourage the innate qualities that will make the difference.

> *"When I moved to X bank, I could not believe the difference in the management of people. In my opinion it was just the modern equivalent of a large Victorian textile firm... Employees had little interest in their work and just came to work for the money and felt they had very little say in the running of the firm, despite various initiatives to improve communication and employee involvement."*

Despite all the initiatives outlined, situations like this are all too common. Yet the solution is in the quotation! "Employees **had little interest in their work** and just came to work for the money **and felt they had very little say in the running of the firm**, despite various initiatives to improve communication and employee involvement."

You see, despite their intentions, the bank had failed to create joy and thus to engender "devotion", and ultimately optimum performance can only come from devotion.

While creating devotion is clearly a complex topic, it is rooted in self-expression. More than interest and involvement, it requires identification with the ownership of their work on the part of employees. Ironically this is synonymous with the fourth of Maslow's five original hierarchical needs (Esteem) and so it would appear that we have not learned much in the past 60 years!

Any parent will identify with the small child who wants to do something by himself or herself, without any adult interference. Yet this is a characteristic that we all take with us throughout our lives. If we have a task to do, we will try to do it ourselves and only ask for assistance if or when we need it.[1]

But there is more to it than that. Just as a child may throw a tantrum or refuse to co-operate or even try to complete a task when an adult starts to help, we as adults also resent unsolicited help. The more we are told what to do, the more we see it as interference or meddling. This undermines our independence and consequently our self-esteem, and thus certainly takes away any sense of fulfilment rather than adding to it. However, it has a double whammy effect, for it also undermines the amount of effort we put in.

In the introduction I pointed out that a major problem with management science is that we have no concept of how inefficient our use of human capital is, or how much of our potential we are losing. I am convinced that this is one of the

---

[1] Of course there is the cliché about men who will never stop to ask for directions until they are truly, hopelessly lost, but I am not going down that road, and will assume a universal recognition of the point where help is needed and a willingness exists to ask for it or accept it when offered!

major causes of inefficiency and, while I still cannot quantify it, I do have some ideas as to how the topic can be looked at somewhat more empirically, which I would like to share.

THE OBVIOUS

Let me begin by stating the obvious.

Inertia = 0

In the words from the 'Sound of Music': *"Nothing comes from nothing; nothing ever could."* Consequences only result from actions. Without action, there can be no consequences.

Now action is defined in part as "the effecting of an alteration by means of force or some natural power" (Webster). Thus, action is itself a result – the consequence of activity, which by definition is the active agent of force or power. Thus, before anything can happen, some kind of force has to be used. And basic physics teaches us that force is the use of energy, i.e.

Force = Energy expended (Exertion) [2]

---

[2] My recollection of basic physics is that force is a function of mass and acceleration, which is in turn a function of time and motion. Since for the purposes of this discussion we can disregard mass, it is not stretching logic to say that force, exertion and effort can be used interchangeably.

This means that, for any activity, energy has to be expended – that there is some sort of exertion, or effort. Thus:

$$Exertion > 0$$

Since the action is enabled by the exertion, in any given situation the energy used is equivalent to the effort expended, i.e.:

$$Energy\ expended\ (Exertion) = Effort$$

Furthermore, since it can be generally assumed that no action takes place without purpose, we can now see that:

$$Purpose + Effort = Activity$$

Or, to put it another way, activity is the expenditure of energy for a desired purpose. If the purpose is achieved then the outcome or result of the activity is success. Thus:

$$If:\ Outcome > Purpose,$$
$$Then:\ Activity = Success$$

DIGGING A LITTLE DEEPER

Of course, these are very simple logic equations and take no account of any qualitative or quantitative measures which can have a profound effect on the results.

A successful outcome may, just like the internal combustion engine in the introduction, disguise the fact that an inappropriate amount of energy has been used. We all know that a sledgehammer can be used to crack a nut, but that entails an excessive use of force, which could result in the nut being crushed. Thus, there are two additional facts to be noted here:

a) Unnecessary energy has been used.

b) The risk of an outcome other than that desired is greatly increased.

While the prognosis expounded earlier, that "energy expended = effort" may hold true generally, from a personal perspective this is not necessarily always the case. In fact it is most unlikely. Empirically, the result of two people doing exactly the same task may not be the same. Remember, force is a function of time and motion and so, if the ratio of these elements varies, the effort will be different even though the end result is perceived to be the same. Such differences are inevitable when dealing with human beings because, with people, activity is considerably more difficult to replicate exactly, as people are both physically and psychologically different.

This means that a desired outcome is not necessarily always achieved as a result of the same human energy or effort. This introduces a whole new dynamic whilst simultaneously providing a basic insight into the concept of efficiency, for example:

Efficiency = Success achieved for the minimum effort

Basic economics demands operating at maximum efficiency, and it is therefore a truism to say that any organisation, regardless of its nature, is striving to do so; struggling to achieve the desired results from the minimum effort. Thus, all will make appropriate investments to improve performance. Yet unfortunately, because people are more complex, there is little constructive analysis of the human effort and the equivalent investment is seldom if ever made in human capital.

THE FIRST "LAW" OF PERSONAL ENERGY

We notice the expenditure of personal energy far more when doing something we do not enjoy than when we are doing something we enjoy.

This makes "effort" considerably more subjective whilst also having a possible bearing on the amount of energy that is actually expended. People who enjoy an activity will likely be more "diligent" and thus "exert" themselves more than those who do not.

Thus it is possible to derive two different formulae for the same activity:

Activity + Enjoyment = Pleasure
Activity - Enjoyment = Pain

This creates a paradox, as a pleasurable exercise is going to appear less of an effort to someone who finds it so than someone who finds it painful. Yet the actual energy used may be identical to, or even greater than, that used by the latter. As we all know only too well, it is very difficult to apply oneself to something that one does not enjoy. The paradox, however, lies in the fact that the former is somehow able to do even more and thus achieve more noticeable results than the person who theoretically has more energy to spare.

Naturally this also depends on the nature of the task and the person. There may conceivably be times when the opposite applies and additional effort is made to get the job "over-and-done-with" as quickly as possible. For example, I was the fastest finisher of a long distance race you ever saw – simply because by the time the end was finally in sight I was desperate to end my agony!

Some organisations appear to have recognised this, and thus they promote a "fun place to work" ethos, yet the extent to which this actually flows down to an individual employee level is certainly questionable. Nevertheless, it is at least a start and there are far too many organisations that haven't yet begun this evolutionary ascent.

PERFORMANCE MEASUREMENT

It is very simple to point out that efficiency is outcome that involves the least effort, but measuring human effort presents an almost impossible mission. While it is possible to empirically measure and monitor performance through benchmarking and other such techniques, these are still only a comparative measure, and not an assessment of what is possible for the individual concerned - merely approximating what is possible.

Not only do people have different capabilities that make comparisons difficult, but they may be operating in different environments with different constraints that make such yardsticks meaningless.

Even if it were possible to somehow measure the intellectual and physical potential of an individual employee and accurately monitor, measure and record their mental and physical effort on an ongoing basis (something that might make slave labour look positively benign!) there are all the psychological issues that come into play which further distort the measurement model, and which effectively erode any ability to realistically assess effort.

The first law of personal energy clearly illustrates that these psychological elements are a significant factor, but they have particularly important implications when people are juggling their different life roles and the inherent conflict in trying to do justice to them all. Any over-exertion in one role is inevitably at the expense of others, but if the over-exertion is in fact only a perceived state of affairs rather than a real one, the situation is further complicated, because it contains the seeds of future conflict for which there may be no visible warning signs.

Ironically, these unmeasured psychological issues are probably the most significant factor of all in determining the degree of exertion. Regardless of what others may consider the appropriate amount of effort to put into a job or role, it is ultimately only the individual who can really decide. This will be a personal decision, based on the degree to which it satisfies their esteem and self-actualisation needs, and/or their perception of their effectiveness in dealing with their multiple roles.

So while attempts to make the workplace fun are laudable, they are inevitably limited since they perpetuate the old top-down school of management and try to prescribe a collective concept of what fun is, which can never take account of all the factors which determine the effort an individual will make.

Once again it is apparent that the whole issue is best left to the individual to manage for themselves, within parameters of agreed expectations. Any attempt to compel effort, whether through tangible incentives, stretch targets or any other means, will only have a short-term effect and may prove counter-productive in the longer term. The employer's role is simply to provide the environment and support that will allow a person to self-manage more effectively. For example:

Two young audit clerks were working overtime one weekend, checking inventory at an iron foundry, and were told that in order to validate the reliability of the stock records they each needed to take 25 items of significant value from the yard and check them against the system, and then take 25 items from the system and physically verify their existence.

It was a cold day, and they both had other things that they would rather have been doing, and counting sheets of metal and pieces of angle iron in a freezing warehouse was never going to be fun. So in order to make it bearable, they decided to have a wager as to who would finish first.

Now, being potentially good auditors, they knew they had to have some sort of check that the job had been done properly, so it was agreed that, once they had completed the task, they would sample test one-another's count to ensure it had been done properly, and that any discrepancies would invalidate the bet.

Thus the work was:

- Carried out as quickly as possible.
- Conducted with the utmost care.
- Independently (and strictly speaking unnecessarily) quality controlled.
- Finished nearly an hour sooner than anticipated.

Do you think that any traditional top-down efforts of the audit manager to achieve this would have been as effective?

It may be difficult to positively measure performance, but there are certainly negative measures that provide a clear indication of individual and organisational malfunction and the need for improvement. The three most significant are:

- Poor productivity
- Management/staff conflict
- Shoddy customer service

Satisfied people – those enjoying their work – will inevitably take more interest in their work; "go the extra mile" to help customers and support their colleagues.

Thus the key is to move beyond incentives and find a way to create role ownership, whereby people are able to find the link between their inner self and their work. This will create commitment and enthusiasm, and thus spark devotion and stimulate greater effort. This is starting down the track of fulfilment and the development of the "F" we were talking about earlier.

CHAPTER 4

BEYOND ENERGY

"That state is a state of slavery in which a man does what he likes to do in his spare time and in his working time that which is required of him."

Eric Gill: Sculptor and Typographer, 1882-1940

The message that employees should be allowed to take more responsibility for their own positions should be becoming increasingly clear.

Every indicator of higher performance points in that direction, and we have just seen that people are more likely to expend more effort on activities they enjoy, and be their own best judges of their effort.

This is not a new message. All leading pundits on successful future organisations state the need for "helping people become more powerful". It is really a case of enlightened self-interest or selfish altruism – a variant of the Golden Rule:

"Do unto others as ye would have them do unto you."

It recognises that: "Before you ask people to *do* something you have to help them *be* something".

As we have seen, doing anything – even getting out of bed in the morning – takes energy. When asking people to do something we are asking them to expend their energy. So surely it is a no-brainer that they will be more willing to do so if the activity is aligned with their own "self-interest"?

Yet despite this, many people, if not most, spend their lives in that state of slavery depicted in the above quote. This has to change if organisations are to succeed. After all, an organisation is, by definition, a collection of individuals.

*"In the end, an organisation is nothing more than the **collective capacity** of its people to create value."* (Lou Gerstner, former Chairman and CEO of IBM.) Therefore, the greater the capacity of the individual, the greater the collective capacity: organisational success ultimately depends on individual effort. Therefore:

- The starting point has to be the individual.
- There has to be alignment between personal and organisational objectives.

PERSONAL DEVELOPMENT

If success is dependent on the individual, it necessarily follows that the greater the personal development the greater the likelihood of organisational success. The better an employee can "be", the greater their value to the organisation.

So we need to look a little more closely at personal development.

While there are a number of factors that determine how people develop, they can ultimately be broadly distilled into two main, mutually dependent elements:

- Attitude.
- Ability – a conglomeration of talent, training, experience and skill.

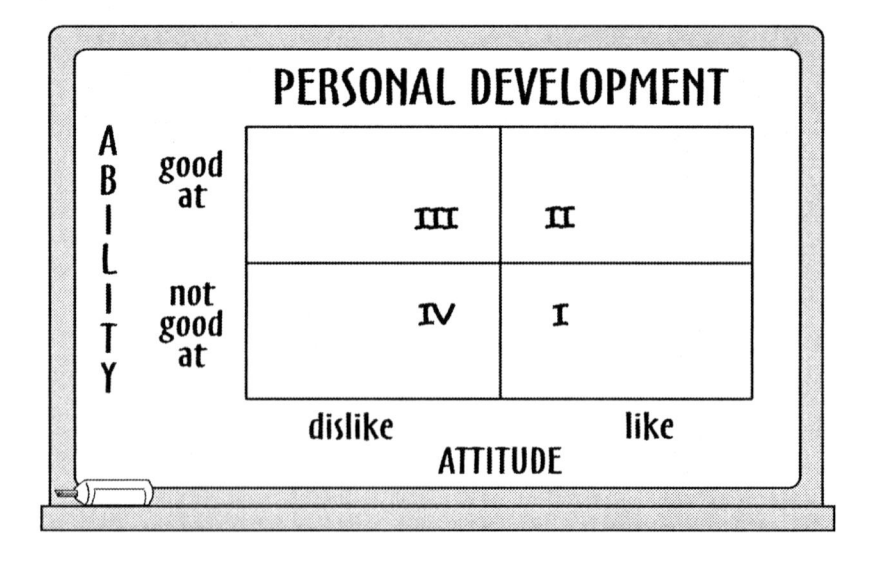

PERSONAL DEVELOPMENT

	dislike	like
ABILITY good at	III	II
ABILITY not good at	IV	I

ATTITUDE

Plotting against these two elements enables us to create a traditional four-quadrant matrix, as follows.

These quadrants (as anyone familiar with matrix development would expect) can each be uniquely identified to generically depict a person's state of mind.

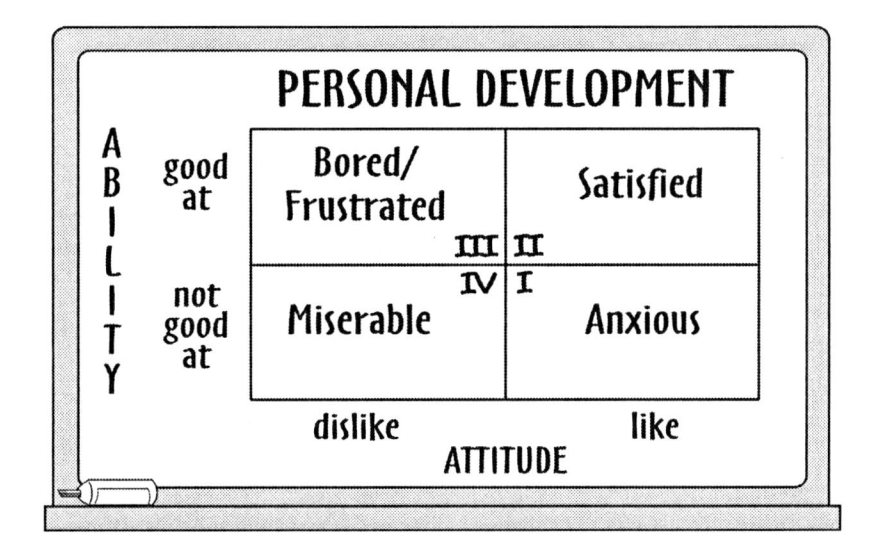

PERSONAL DEVELOPMENT

	ATTITUDE	
	dislike	like
ABILITY good at	Bored/Frustrated (III)	Satisfied (II)
ABILITY not good at	Miserable (IV)	Anxious (I)

As you look at each quadrant, the points to remember are:

- An individual does not remain static, but changes over time.

- A person develops an interest in something and starts to build on it.

- Initially, people are not very good at new skills and feel anxious, but with time and practice their ability develops.

- As they gain more experience, they move into the second quadrant and start feeling satisfied.

If they continue with the activity, as more time elapses and they find they have achieved their highest level of attainment, they start to become bored and/or frustrated with the activity.

Sometimes called "rustout" (as the opposite of "burnout"), this starts to create a downward spiral in which their performance actually begins to deteriorate.

If they persist with the activity, this can take them full circle into the fourth quadrant, where they hate the activity and can ultimately even become totally incompetent, or else, as has been known to happen on production lines in mass production factories, they start to take out their resentment and frustration by actually resorting to sabotage.

This "Doom Loop" – first described by Dr Dory Hollander in her book "The Doom Loop System" published in 1991 – is depicted in the following chart.

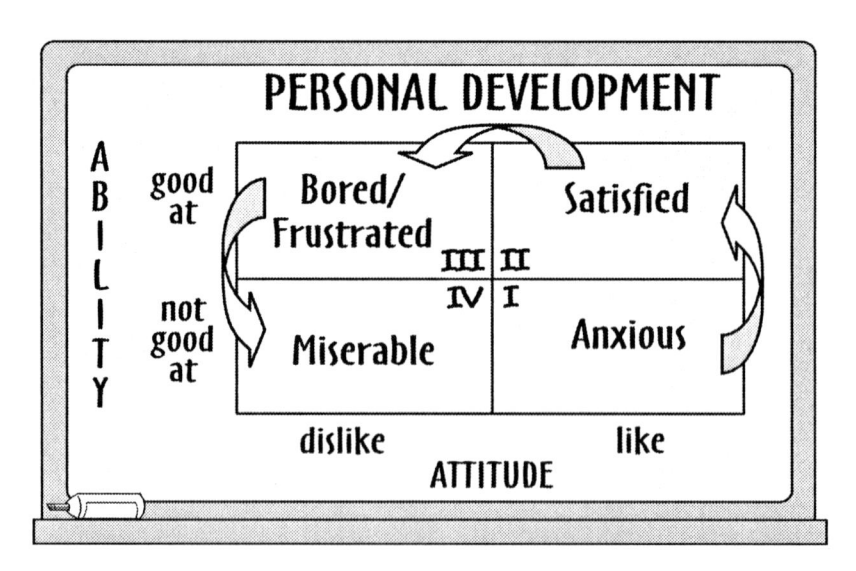

PERSONAL DEVELOPMENT

ABILITY	Attitude: dislike	Attitude: like
good at	Bored/Frustrated (III)	Satisfied (II)
not good at	Miserable (IV)	Anxious (I)

THE "DOOM LOOP"

This obviously has major implications for people at work, and can perhaps be better understood when one looks at it in the context of the expenditure of energy.

How often has one seen the work of high performers start to tail off, seemingly inexplicably? Seen in this new light, this is no longer quite so mysterious. After all, everyone knows how boredom leads to listlessness and ennui. Why should anyone think this does not apply in a work situation too?

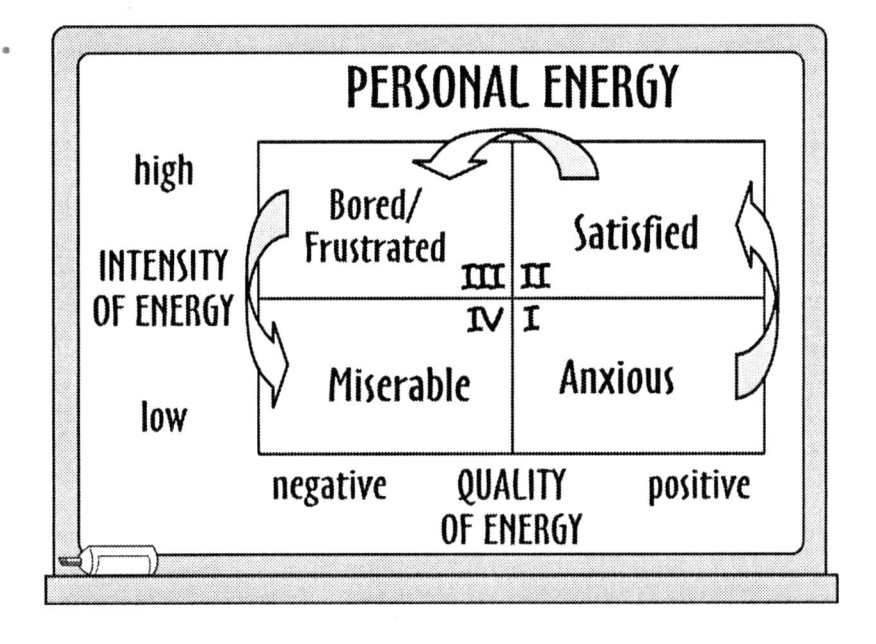

PERSONAL ENERGY

	negative	positive
high intensity	Bored/Frustrated (III)	Satisfied (II)
low intensity	Miserable (IV)	Anxious (I)

INTENSITY OF ENERGY (high / low) — QUALITY OF ENERGY (negative / positive)

The real tragedy of this situation is not just that this syndrome frequently remains unrecognised by employers, but often also by employees themselves. This is because of the psychological effects associated with energy described earlier.

Since applying oneself to something that one does not enjoy seems to use up more energy, we often think we are working just as hard if not harder long after our interest has waned. Consequently it can come as a bolt from the blue to the employee to learn that their performance has deteriorated.

SELECTION AND RECRUITMENT FAILURE

This doom loop is universal and undermines the efforts of all, from the complaints clerk who deals with numerous customer complaints that are rooted in poor systems and processes that they are unable to change, to the workaholic executive who suddenly starts to experience a mid-life crisis.

Clearly personal fulfilment is critical to higher performance at all levels. Yet, by-and-large, Human Resources functions appear to have remained oblivious to this phenomenon.

What this ignorance has contributed to employee turnover rates can only be surmised, but what is an even more disturbing aspect is that the phenomenon is perpetuated in the whole hiring process.

Recruitment begins with a job description and a list of characteristics required for a particular role, and recruiters set out to find a candidate who fits the bill. Consequently they will not only (probably rightly) reject a candidate who has more than the ten things required per their list as overqualified for the job, but they will also reject the candidate who only has nine as being under-qualified for the job. This means that when they actually do find their "ideal" candidate they are actually recruiting someone who is virtually at the top of the doom loop cycle!

Thus, while the stimulus of a new environment and new colleagues to impress gives the successful candidate the energy to thrive in the first few months, creating a "new brooms sweep clean" impression, it is purely a matter of time before they start to move into the bored/frustrated quadrant.

The proof of this lies in the fact that, even when the "ideal" candidate cannot be found, the job still gets done somehow. And I am sure most people can cite examples of people who, having been "thrown in at the deep-end", have managed to exceed all expectations. Surely, however, this simply underscores John Steinbeck's earlier observation:

"It is the nature of man to rise to greatness if greatness is expected of him."

Failure to recognise this concept results in wastage. Unfortunately, this prevailing attitude means that new staff and old alike are all at risk of operating from the downward cycle of the doom loop, hardly something likely to contribute to the long-term success of the organisation.

UNLEASHING ORGANISATIONAL ENERGY

With the micro-level organisational energy picture looking that bleak, the challenge to create effective macro-level energy is likely to be extremely daunting. After all, people unconsciously respond to one-another's emotional displays by imitating or exaggerating them. So, if the majority are uninspired, the "disease" is likely to be contagious and have a profound effect on the organisation.

An article "Unleashing Organisational Energy" in the MIT/Sloan Fall 2003 Review illustrates this point and effectively shows a modified form of the personal energy matrix, as follows.

The quadrants, as you would expect, are very similar, although I have used the names given to them in the Sloan article.

ORGANISATIONAL ENERGY

	negative QUALITY OF ENERGY positive	
INTENSITY OF ENERGY high	Aggression Zone	Passion Zone
low	Resignation Zone	Comfort Zone

The basic difference on an organisational level is that without specific initiatives to drive them in the opposite direction, the doom loop forces tend to have a gravitational effect that pulls the energy levels down. This is depicted in the next chart:

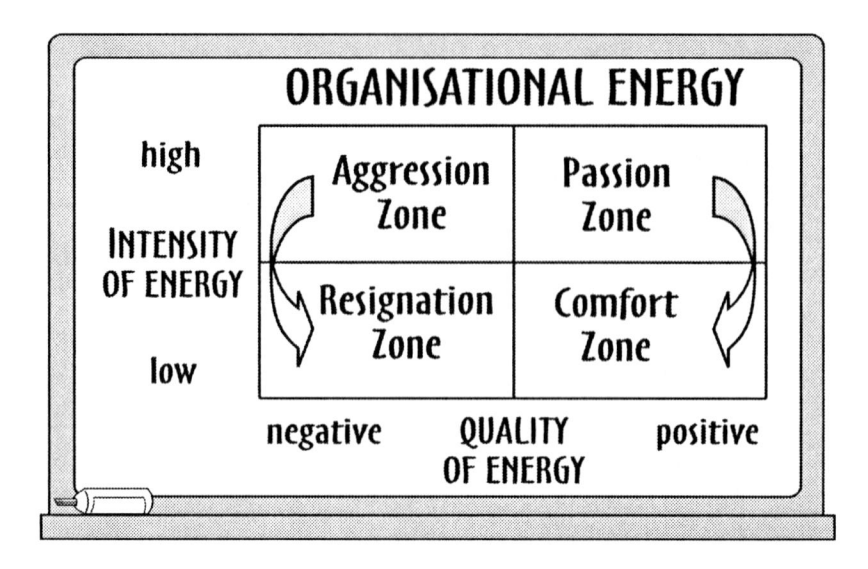

ORGANISATIONAL ENERGY

	negative	positive
high INTENSITY OF ENERGY	Aggression Zone	Passion Zone
low	Resignation Zone	Comfort Zone

QUALITY OF ENERGY

So, if you are an executive in any organisation you need to be aware of this and recognise that you have a challenge to counter this effect. How? Well, the article points out that there are basically two options: "Slaying the Dragon" and "Winning the Princess". These can be depicted as follows:

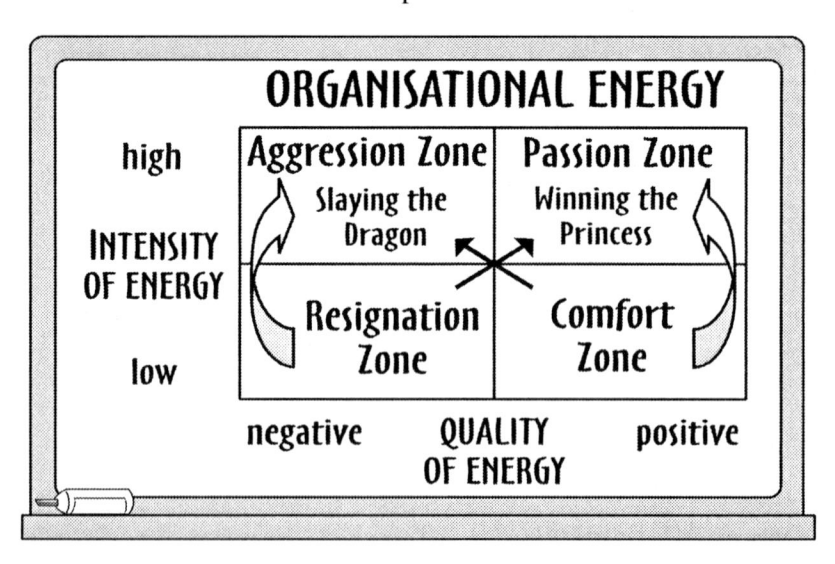

ORGANISATIONAL ENERGY

	negative	positive
high INTENSITY OF ENERGY	Aggression Zone — Slaying the Dragon	Passion Zone — Winning the Princess
low	Resignation Zone	Comfort Zone

QUALITY OF ENERGY

REMEDIAL STRATEGIES

While it might be ideal to combine the "Slaying the Dragon" with "Winning the Princess", these two strategies actually tend to be mutually exclusive; after all, no one is particularly worried about the princess when the dragon is scorching their backsides. Contradictions and ambiguities inherent in integrating the strategies might lead to the worst of all worlds in which neither works.

SLAYING THE DRAGON

This entails invoking an organisational response to an external and significant threat. As such it requires:

- A visible threat that is personal and that jeopardises the organisation and all its stakeholders.
- A disciplined process that must channel emotions.
- Leaders to guide, monitor and control the process.

As depicted, it is generally more appropriate to move employees from the resignation zone into the aggression zone, but it can also be used to move into the passion zone.

WINNING THE PRINCESS

This entails shifting the organisational values and, as it is much more inspirational, it requires:

- Defining, describing and substantiating something intangible but meaningful.
- Leaders that embody the vision.
- Leaders to balance pursuit of the vision with protecting the ongoing business.

BEYOND ENERGY

It should be clear that the former is a strategy that channels energy as a result of a potentially negative outcome and thus feeds on negative emotions, while the latter involves a more positive response through channelling positive emotions.

This is why they tend to be mutually exclusive, but both are difficult to sustain for the long term because the energy they invoke dissipates once the objective is attained.

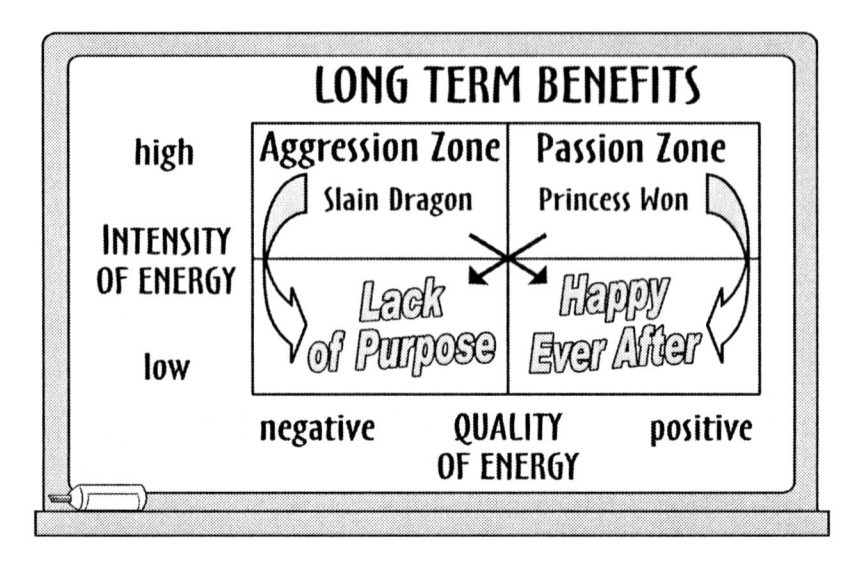

LONG TERM BENEFITS

	Aggression Zone	Passion Zone
high INTENSITY OF ENERGY low	Slain Dragon	Princess Won
	Lack of Purpose	Happy Ever After

negative — QUALITY OF ENERGY — positive

We all know that once the princess has been won, everyone lives happily ever after, which clearly moves the organisation into the comfort zone. Similarly, once the dragon is slain, there is a lack of purpose which means that things will slip back to the way they were before the threat was exposed. It is unlikely that an organisation will revert to the comfort zone after the dragon is slain, unless it was in that zone before the dragon was identified, and even more unlikely that it will move into the resignation zone after the princess was won, simply because of the positive effect of winning the princess.

CREATING LASTING ENERGY

Since these strategies will deliver no lasting benefits one is compelled to ask if there is any way to create lasting, long-term energy. Clearly the challenge is one that executives have to be constantly alert to, but the answer is yes. However, it means going back to where we started – to the individual. Evidently, the challenge is to "stay on the right side" and keep employees from dropping down the back of the doom loop, thus ensuring that they retain and renew their enthusiasm.

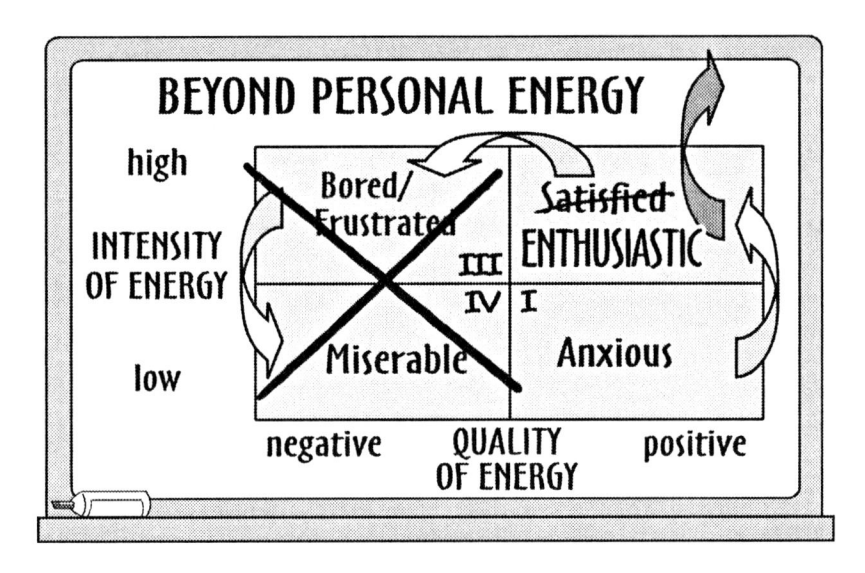

BEYOND PERSONAL ENERGY

INTENSITY OF ENERGY: high / low
QUALITY OF ENERGY: negative / positive

- III: Bored/Frustrated (crossed out)
- II: Satisfied / ENTHUSIASTIC
- IV: Miserable (crossed out)
- I: Anxious

This is tantamount to regarding the individual as being on a personal continuous improvement path. Surely this should be obvious in any "learning organisation" that is striving for continuous improvement, but there is scant evidence of it in the commercial world at large. In fact, this is synonymous with seeing employees as having a "job-life cycle" where each point in which the employee starts to move down the doom loop represents the end of a "job-life" and is the point where something needs to be done to rekindle enthusiasm or engender some new training programme that will allow the employee to further develop.

Andre Grove of Intel said: "*There is at least one moment in the history of any company when you have to change dramatically to reach the next level of performance. Miss the moment and you start to decline.*" The same is true of employee performance, with the only difference being that there will definitely be more than one moment (as is increasingly likely for companies too).

This can be depicted on a classic life-cycle S curve, and here too, Charles Handy's words about corporate development apply equally to the individual: *"The way you get continued growth in the future is by building a new curve before the first one begins to descend, which means being constantly inventive and creative."*

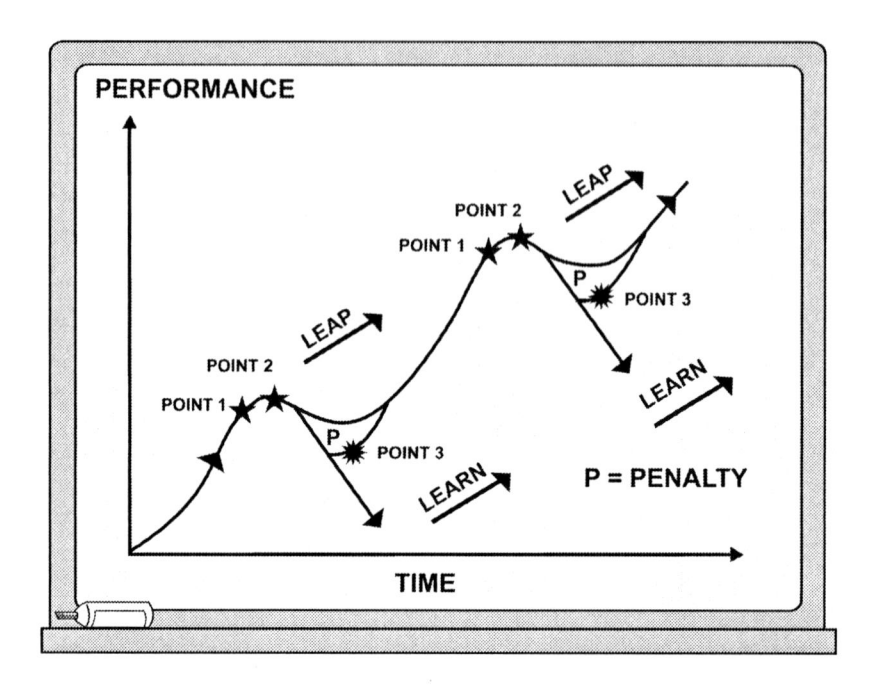

[Figure: Performance vs Time diagram showing two overlapping S-curves. The first curve has POINT 1, POINT 2 (with LEAP arrow), P (PENALTY), POINT 3, and LEARN arrow. The second curve repeats the same pattern at a higher level. P = PENALTY]

Ideally one should "take the leap" and start to find some way to improve either the role or the person's capability somewhere between Points 1 and 2, in order to allow the person to make the leap onto the new learning curve. After moving beyond Point 2 there is a cost to the organisation in effectiveness and efficiency. If you reach Point 3 you are already in crisis. By recognising and understanding these points, and acting accordingly, you will be able to:

- Let your employees be the best they can be and give them the scope to take responsibility for their own development whilst aligning their personal development with the goals of the organisation.

- Create personal energy levels that act as a dynamo to fellow employees.

- Unleash the organisational energy your organisation needs to function in the fast-changing environment of the 21st century.

- Super-charge your organisation's success.

I have proved this in my own experience. Some years ago I was employed by a leading life assurance company to help resolve problems with data integrity. It was in the early days of commercial computers and the company had undergone a massive computerisation programme. Unfortunately, the key performance measure for IT projects was whether or not it was completed on time. This led to short-cuts being taken in testing which, compounded by poor initial specification in which the financial and control requirements had not been considered, meant that things were starting to spiral out of control and the company's reputation was being damaged amongst policy holders and brokers as a result of inaccurate policy information.

My strategy to address this problem was to recruit a team of accountants with computer experience to work with IT and users to improve the systems and prevent further problems, while a separate team worked on cleaning up the corrupt data. This strategy was accepted by the executive management team, but resisted by the Human Resources department who:

- Were unwilling to recruit outside the standard salary bands.

- Maintained that it would be impossible to retain such high calibre professionals even if they could be recruited.

The first obstacle was simply overcome by a CEO mandate to create a new professional salary band, but the second presented a significant challenge, particularly since none of the recruits had any previous experience of the life assurance industry.

Determined to prove HR wrong, I developed a strong tactical plan whereby:

- Systems development standards were amended to stipulate that in future there had to be a representative from Finance on all IT projects.
- Each team member was assigned responsibility for one of the primary operating divisions in the company, meaning that they were responsible for all significant systems development within that division.
- Each team member was assigned a secondary responsibility for one of the other divisions, meaning that they had to provide understudy support to their colleagues, whilst also working on smaller projects to spread the workload.
- Regular departmental meetings were held at which they had to report on each of the projects in which they were involved, explaining what was being done, why, and what controls they were implementing.

Not only did this approach help ensure that each of them got to understand all aspects of the business, but it gave them a span of control and a sense of responsibility that was truly fulfilling. This ensured that not only was my mandate met considerably earlier than anticipated, but each of them was retained for the duration and made such an impression within the organisation that they were snapped up for promotion elsewhere in the company when the opportunity arose – as I had promised they would be.

Truly, creating fulfilment is the first step in building FAT employees that have an energising effect on the whole organisation.

CHAPTER 5

'A' IS FOR AWARENESS AND ALIGNMENT

Now, it is all very well having a bunch of enthusiastic, energised, self-motivated people running about the place, but that on its own can be a recipe for disaster. We have all experienced occasions when – even with the best intentions in the world – personal drive and enthusiasm for the cause have led to conflict and confusion, with nothing being achieved and goodwill and endeavour being replaced by anger and apathy. If chaos is to be avoided, we have to ensure that there is proper alignment of both purpose and process. Such alignment entails bringing together the personal and the organisational objectives.

Inevitably this has to start with the individual. The individual has to know:

- Who they are
- What they are
- What they can do
- What they want to do
- How they can progress
- What they have to do to progress

This is basically self-awareness and as such is, or should be, obvious and integral to our lives. Yet, I suspect it is a lot less common than it should be, for two reasons:

1. It is often more sub-conscious than conscious. As we all get caught up in the routine of our daily lives, this ongoing self-appraisal becomes sublimated.

2. We are all constrained by our job-descriptions that not only distort our self-perception, but actually start to dictate our development path.

Statistical evidence shows that people with plans are more successful than those without, but for many the consequence of things not going to plan is to simply stop planning. Because successful planning is rooted in self-awareness, as we become disenchanted with the pattern of our lives our natural defence mechanisms start to kick in and stop us examining our lives too closely.

This effect is compounded by an employment environment that looks upon people as resources to fulfil a specific defined role, rather than as people. Thus, the organisation has to change its approach too, and by seeing and treating people as assets they will not only help rekindle personal self-awareness, but become more aware themselves of the capabilities of their people and thus facilitate an environment of personal development that will inevitably benefit the organisation as well.

A Side Issue

There are definite signs that organisations are aware of this shortcoming and taking steps to address it. One of these is perhaps the increasing promotion of the concept of "work-life balance". This phrase has become de rigueur in HR circles and is at the vanguard of efforts to motivate employees. It is an attempt by management to convince employees that traditional labour practices have been seen to be exploitive and that management now recognises that people do have more to their lives than just their jobs, and that these requirements will be considered when defining the terms of employment for staff. For heaven's sake let us put an end to this concept once and for all, for it is both patronising and counter-productive! What it does is divide a person's life into 2 parts – work and life – and thus implies that they are either working or living. Consequently the two then become competing elements. Of course that is not the intention, but just picture it!

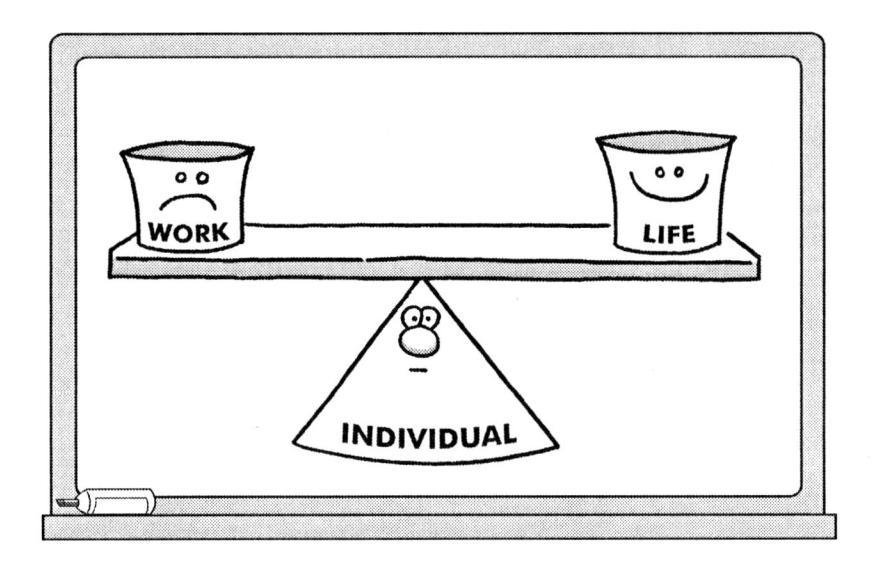

[Illustration: A balance/seesaw on a whiteboard with a "WORK" bucket (sad face) on the left and a "LIFE" bucket (happy face) on the right, resting on a triangular fulcrum labelled "INDIVIDUAL".]

The very term "balance" conjures up a precarious state of equilibrium with a beam resting at the horizontal on a fulcrum. The words "work" and "life" invoke the additional image of two weights resting at either end of the beam. Consequently, there is an inevitable separation and the two are seen as distinctive elements, which the individual has to align in order to keep the whole in balance.

Creating this degree of separation simultaneously creates an intrinsic conflict between the two, which inevitably causes stress when the balance is disturbed. This compels the employee in such a situation to make a choice that ultimately boils down to being between work and life. If they choose life, their work situation will change -either their role/employer will have to change or else the employer will feel exploited and thus consciously or unconsciously experience a change of attitude towards the employee. If they choose work, there will be consequences in their life which they will likely come to resent over time and which will thus impact upon their long-term performance. So either way, the net result is almost invariably a no-win situation for both parties.

It makes work and life appear to be opposites and, since the opposite of life is death, it effectively makes work synonymous with death and reinforces the perception that work is a necessary evil that deprives one of (a) life. Thus it creates an attitude whereby work is something that, wherever possible, should be avoided. Of course I understand that the phrase "work-life balance" is just a term and that it is the situation that gives rise to the problem, not the term. The crux of the issue is that using the term perpetuates an image of conflict. It effectively reinforces the perception that work is a necessary evil that detracts from life. Thus it creates an attitude whereby work is something that, wherever possible, should be avoided.

This generates a kind of schizophrenia that is hardly conducive to greater productivity and the development of the esteem and ownership that is essential to creating greater awareness, ownership and devotion. Indeed it perpetuates that very state of slavery depicted by Eric Gill that we are trying to redress.

"Work is love made visible. And if you cannot work with love, but only with distaste, it is better that you should leave your work and sit at the gate of the temple and take alms of those who work with joy." Kahlil Gibran

This quotation puts it more beautifully than I ever could. The point, though, is that work is an integral part of our lives. If we separate work and life we are effectively shortchanging ourselves. The key is to create a greater union between the two, which will in turn help us to move up Maslow's Hierarchy and achieve greater fulfilment and self-actualisation.

ROLE CONFLICT

This is not to stick our heads in the clouds and pretend that there is not a problem of juggling different responsibilities in our lives, which is a problem that causes practical difficulties for each one of us day-by-day. Stephen Covey identified the key to this in his book "7 Habits of Highly Effective People." He pointed out that every one of us has a number of different roles to play – son/daughter, brother/sister, husband/wife, mother/father, employee, friend, etc. – and that each one of us has to recognise these roles and plan and live accordingly, fitting each role into our lives in the way that suits us best. There is inherent conflict in satisfying one particular role simply because of the demands of the others. Even women, with all their multi-tasking capabilities that we lesser mortals lack, can still only play one role effectively at any time.

Covey has provided some very effective solutions to managing this role conflict and it would be pointless and futile for me to attempt to say anything more on the subject. All I would say is that we can better fulfil all our roles if we are happy in our "employment" role. (Of course all roles require "work".) So, we need to find employment that:

- Enables us to best express who and what we are.

- Fits in with our other roles. To the extent that we do the former, the more easily the latter will be achieved.

Ultimately, that is what this book is all about, but it also why awareness is so critically important.

EXPANDING THE "A" FACTOR

In the last chapter, I introduced you to the doom loop and showed how that could impact on personal performance and undermine organisational energy. I also introduced you to the concept of the "job-life cycle" and the S-curve of personal development, and gave you an example of how that contributed to the "F" factor of fulfilment. Now we are looking at the "A" factor. We have just seen the importance of awareness, but have agreed that it has limited value unless employees are ready to commit to working with you on this and there is proper alignment. So now I am going to take you beyond personal development to superior performance through what I call "The Stairway to Stardom".

PRELIMINARY OBSERVATIONS

Personal development is a lifelong process that begins the moment we are born and continues until we die, and the extent to which one continues to actively pursue knowledge and improvement will ultimately determine how close one comes to reaching that nebulous concept of "one's potential". There is no doubting that most people are capable of considerably more than they actually achieve, but personal potential can be measured by both breadth and depth of experience, and the ultimate yardstick can only be that of opportunities that are taken.

Thus, it is ultimately the result of a whole series of smaller developments which brings us back to Stephen Covey's premise concerning the number of roles in life we have. The final judgement has to be against the total person – the way we fulfilled each of these – and is ultimately something between our maker and us.

However, it is inescapable that each of us will achieve more if we align our work development with our overall persona and thus minimise the boundaries between the different roles and the inherent conflict they create. Thus, creating a partnership between the employer and employee will maximise the personal development of the individual in a manner which will enable them to do a better job whilst simultaneously becoming a more fulfilled person. It is only in very rare circumstances that someone sets out to intentionally do anything other than a good job. Consequently, if performance is anything below expectation it must be because there are barriers preventing it. The fact is that personal performance in a work situation is not solely dependent on the individual.

Similarly, while the individual is ultimately responsible for their own personal development, they can seldom take full control of this at work. If personal development is to be maximised and there is to be greater alignment between the individual's "being" and their work role, the personal development program has to be a partnership between the employee and the organisation. This concept underpins everything in this book, but is essential to efforts to counter the doom loop and ensure a personal life-cycle that follows a continually upward progression.

STAIRWAY TO STARDOM

Development is effectively a measure of progress against any defined activity, and as such has to be assessed in the context of two dimensions – time and effort. This measurement can only begin from the time that one becomes conscious of the need to measure, and thus can be considered to have a starting point of zero. At that point there is a conscious awareness of a need "to do something new", and progress can begin to be assessed against these two elements. This is where one is at the foot of the stairs and the climb begins.

The first step can be called "capability"; it is the intrinsic readiness of the individual to develop beyond the base level they have achieved thus far. It may also include talent, which itself includes an above average capability that minimises the effort required relative to someone else who does not have the same innate capability.

The second step is "training". Here, the individual imbibes knowledge passed on in some form by someone who has already acquired the experience and understanding of what is required.

These two steps bring the person to a landing called "ability". This is a platform that allows the person to launch to the next step and put their new-found knowledge to practical use.

The third step is "experience" which is simply the result of increased comfort at the task as a result of doing it more and more. This, supported by talent, brings the individual to another level called "skill" (or proficiency), whereby they are now able to exploit what they have learned. This is the point at which their ability becomes truly marketable and, if they are not already doing so, they can look to it to earn or increase earnings. It is at this level that the environment in which the skills are applied starts to take on greater significance. This is reflected in the next two steps.

The fourth step is "support". This is where the individual is given credit for their development, and their efforts are acknowledged and encouraged by others who play their part in ensuring that they are properly utilised.

The fifth step is "interference" and is slightly different from any of the previous steps because, where they involve what may be considered as additions in the development equation, the fifth step requires a subtraction – the removal of those factors which prevent

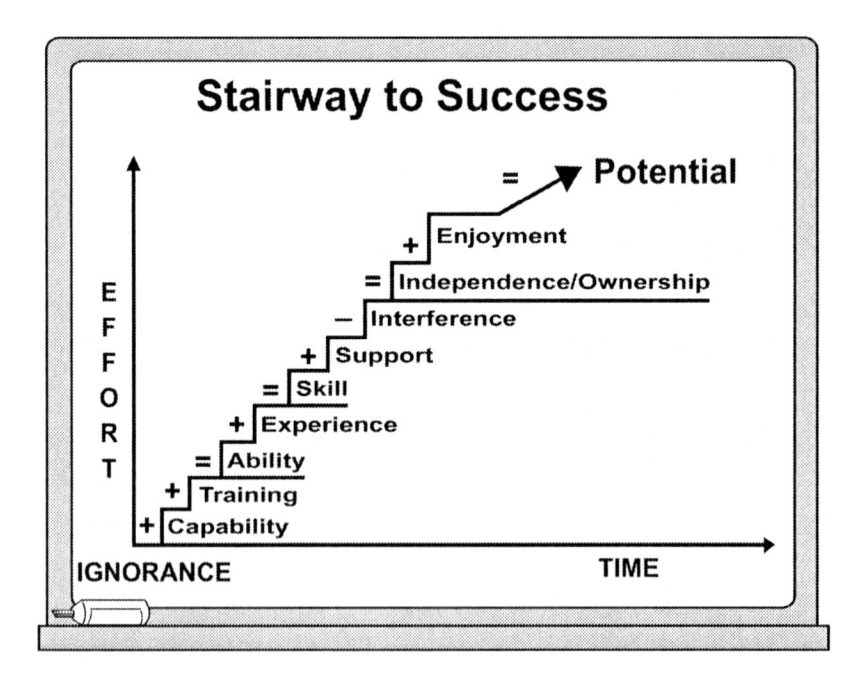

Stairway to Success

EFFORT (y-axis), TIME (x-axis), starting at IGNORANCE

Steps ascending:
- + Capability
- + Training
- = Ability
- + Experience
- = Skill
- + Support
- − Interference
- = Independence/Ownership
- + Enjoyment
- = Potential

the person doing his best and thus creating obstacles to higher level performance.

Steps four and five are complementary and require a fine balance, for too much support or unsolicited support constitutes interference, while too little denotes disinterest or apathy and can also become an obstacle. However, when they are in balance, they create a further landing that I have called "independence" which brings total ownership of the role.

ENJOYMENT TURBO-CHARGES ENTHUSIASM

This in turn engenders the next step – "enthusiasm" – which creates the innate motivation that I referred to earlier. This is because they are enjoying the role and enjoyment turbocharges enthusiasm.

Of course, enthusiasm is what launches the push for further development and drives a quest for continuous improvement that sees the individual embark on a course to break the vicious cycle of the doom loop, enlarge their potential, and increase their self-fulfilment.

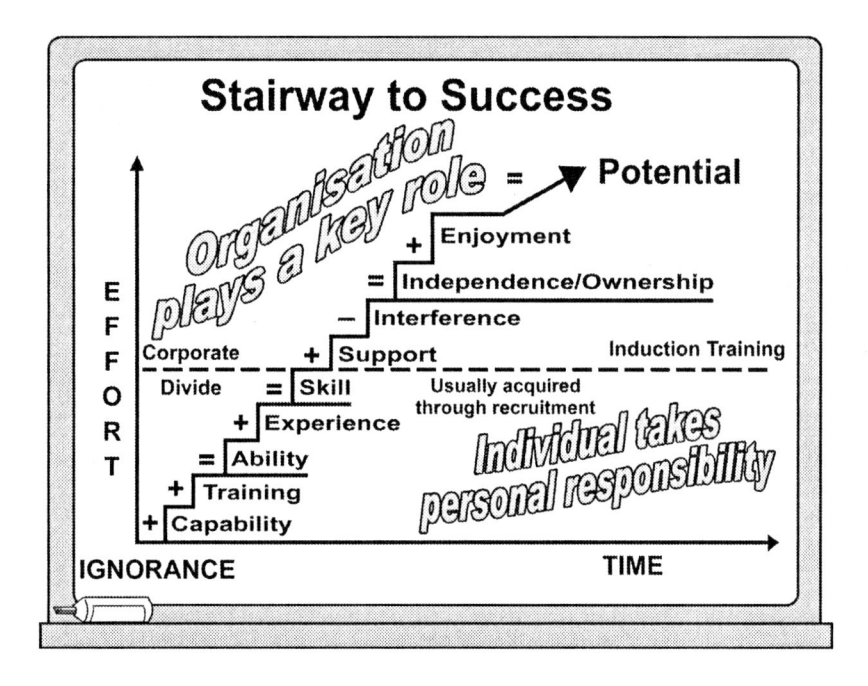

Stairway to Success

Organisation plays a key role

EFFORT

- + Enjoyment = Potential
- = Independence/Ownership
- − Interference
- Corporate + Support — Induction Training
- Divide = Skill — Usually acquired through recruitment
- + Experience
- = Ability
- + Training
- + Capability

Individual takes personal responsibility

IGNORANCE ──────────────────── TIME →

ORGANISATION VS. PERSONAL RESPONSIBILITY

I have already indicated that this development needs to be a partnership between the individual and the organisation. The obvious question however is: "Where does the boundary lie?" When does the onus shift from the individual to the organisation? I believe the general answer is implicit in the stairway itself for, as a general rule, the individual is responsible for developing his or her own skills. The organisation recruits employees based on those skills. This creates the natural divide depicted in the chart on the previous page.

Of course, this is not always the case because an organisation can also be responsible for helping a person obtain skills:

- As part of an apprentice or graduate recruitment scheme.
- When an existing employee moves into a new position that requires a degree of retraining.

At the same time the individual may also identify additional personal development requirements when established in employment either:

- As a valid response to changing circumstances that demand new skills to enable them to do the job better.
- As a step to personal progress -to acquire additional skills to enable them to do more advanced work or fulfil a different role.

This is not radically different from historical perceptions, other than the fact that it all needs to be seen in the context of developing the individual to their maximum and the fact that it should be a collaborative effort. Too often in the past, a more self-interested approach by one or both parties has resulted in any one or more of the following situations:

- The organisation provides training for the individual who promptly uses his newly acquired skill to move to another organisation.

- The organisation provides training as a 'reward' for perceived good performance, with little or no tangible benefit to the organisation. Stories are commonplace of organisations seeing little tangible benefit from their training expenditure.

- Individuals undergoing training in their own time at their own expense – job related or otherwise – that results in their paying diluted attention to their work and, often, leaving immediately after they have achieved their goal.

This clearly has to change and the implementation of a more aligned approach should ensure that it does.

CHAPTER 6

'A' IS ALSO FOR ASSETS

The last chapter illustrated that there is a pressing need for organisations to partner with their people in developing themselves. Now I am going to give you an idea how this can be more effectively done.

CAN PEOPLE BE ASSETS?

Most organisations claim, *"Our people are our most important asset"*. Yet this is invariably a statement that bears challenging. There are several reasons why such statements are at best delusional and at worst downright fraudulent.

[Cartoon: Two workers standing in glue at the ACME GLUE CO. factory. One says: "NOW YOU KNOW WHY THE COMPANY CALLS US FIXED ASSETS..."]

From a purely accounting perspective, the statement that people are an important asset, let alone *the most important asset*, is absolute nonsense. Assets are recorded in an organisation's balance sheet and employees are not included amongst them.

Adam Smith identified the three elements of production, and thus of economic development, as land, labour and capital. Yet, only two of the three appear in the balance sheet; the land and the capital. Does this mean (ignoring the finer points of accounting semantics!) that land and capital are assets but that labour is not? Surely it cannot! Human endeavour is as much a factor of production as the others, and arguably the most significant of the three. So, to leave it out of the picture in this way actually defies logic. The fact that labour has been treated differently is probably quite simply the result of the relative values placed on the three elements historically, when appropriate land and capital were difficult to acquire whereas labour was unskilled and plentiful.

OR ARE THEY SIMPLY AN EXPENSE?

As a result, people were "expendable" and thus, instead of being regarded as an asset, came to be regarded as an expense – an attitude that has not really changed even today, despite the grand hyperbole issuing from boardrooms and published in Chief Executives' and Directors' reports. Evidence of this is readily found in most organisations today when – as soon as times get tough – employee and employee-related costs are amongst the first to be cut. If people were truly the most important asset, surely these costs should be amongst the last to be cut?

Even the logic of reducing staff during a downturn in the business cycle begs the question as to whether or not business managers understand the most basic fundamentals of economics. After all, at a time when you want to improve organisational productivity it hardly makes economic sense to incur expenses that deliver no return whatsoever - which is the true effect of redundancy payments. Nor is the statement that it is necessary "pain for the long-term gain" any more valid, because most organisations immediately start rehiring when the good times return. If they didn't, they would not have to lay off more when the next downturn comes around!

SO WHICH IS IT?

It would seem that management is clearly confused. On one hand they claim that their people are assets but do not treat them as such, while on the other they regard them as an expense and thereby fail to recognise their true nature as a key factor of production. It would seem obvious that it is impossible for any resource to be both an asset and an expense, and so clearly management cannot continue to have it both ways as they have been doing. Clearly a choice needs to be made. Do they opt to continue regarding their people as an expense, with all the anomalies that entails, or do they practice what they preach and start to treat their people as the assets they claim them to be – and redefine traditional accounting practice to accommodate this?

ACCOUNTING FOR PEOPLE

Perhaps there is another reason why people have not been treated as assets. Traditionally assets have an initial purchase price which makes them easy to value and thus to record for balance sheet purposes. On top of that they tend:

- To get "used up" in the production process.
- To become obsolete as technical progress results in more efficient models.
- Both of the above.

As a result, a portion of their cost is treated as an expense and charged to the Profit & Loss Account as depreciation or wear and tear. The amount thus charged is determined by convention and based on estimates of the duration of their usefulness. Yet, the same is not really true of people. For, unlike machines, people can develop over time and increase in value. Consequently, rather than "depreciating", people actually "appreciate" as they become more experienced and acquire new capabilities.

However, it is not quite as simple as that because people require considerably more than machines to keep producing. Furthermore, there is often an additional cost associated with their "improvement" further complicated by the fact that sometimes this is borne by the employer and sometimes by the employee. It is as a result of these complications that we are in the predicament we are in today. It has simply been too difficult to accommodate all these differences, and that is the reason why people costs have been simply regarded as an expense. The question is "Can we afford to continue doing so?"

RETURN ON ASSETS

One of the major consequences of not treating people as assets is that the true productivity and comparative value of the business has never been properly assessed. It used to be that a key business measure was "Return on Assets" – the ratio of profit to the value of the total assets. Over the course of time this changed to be the "Return on Capital Employed" on the basis that the capital employed was equal to the "Total Net Assets" anyway. This measure was perhaps a natural consequence of the over-emphasis of capital as a factor of production as alluded to earlier, but its dominance has perhaps had more serious consequences. This is because, by overlooking assets (through the failure to recognise assets as meaning "factors of production" and thus excluding labour), business has failed completely to identify the true value added of its endeavours. In other words we have been misstating profits ever since the start of the Industrial Revolution.

Of course, there have been initiatives in the past to account for true added value, but it is questionable to what extent these have attempted to address the method of accounting for people – especially at the individual or "micropersonnel" level.

MUTUAL DEPENDENCE vs. CONTRACT OF EMPLOYMENT

A major consequence of this shortcoming – and the pervasive attitude of regarding an employee as a replaceable commodity – has been the contract of employment and its alter ego, the job description. People have been hired (and doesn't that term itself speak volumes for the attitude to employment?) to do a specific job, and that has been the overriding emphasis in the whole contract. The job has been the most important factor and everything has revolved around how well the job has been done. The parameters of the role have been predetermined, and the individual's ability to comply with these has determined the strength of the relationship.

Although career planning and other HR practices have evolved to "smooth the edges" of the relationship, these changes have largely been motivated by the employer's interests and the focus has remained on the specifics of the job rather than on the individual's ability and their true potential. It has been, and remains, a question of moulding a person for the job rather than moulding the job for the person. This results in the employee pretty quickly entering the bored/frustrated quadrant and inevitably into the back end of the doom loop, and a downward spiral from boredom or frustration into misery.

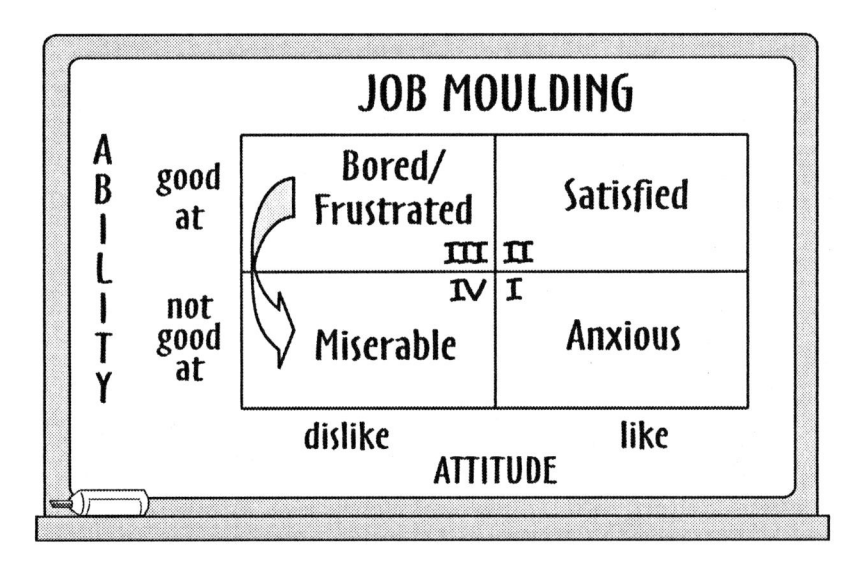

		JOB MOULDING	
A B I L I T Y	good at	Bored/ Frustrated III	Satisfied II
	not good at	Miserable IV	Anxious I
		dislike ATTITUDE	like

Similarly, if enough attention is not paid to the individual and their personal development, an organisation can get itself into a situation where HR policy dictates that personnel changes are based on seniority and length of service, which results in employees being promoted beyond their level of competence, fulfilling the Peter Principle and ultimately disappointing both parties. What happens here is that, after moving into the anxiety quadrant, which is what happens after any change in position, such employees find that they are unable to enhance their ability, either to the level demanded or within the time pressures dictated by the position.

Thus, instead or moving up the positive side of the doom loop, that employee "goes into reverse" and moves back into the miserable quadrant.

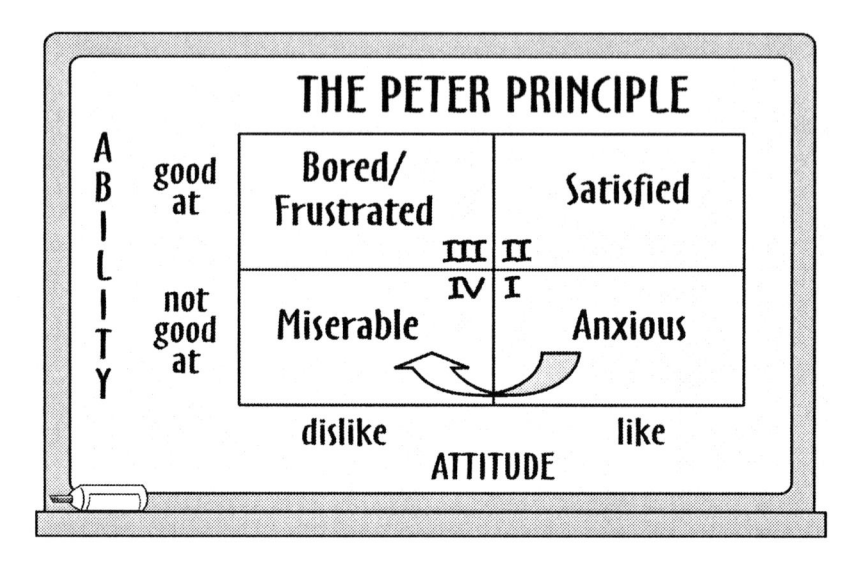

THE PETER PRINCIPLE

	dislike	like
ABILITY good at	Bored/Frustrated (III)	Satisfied (II)
ABILITY not good at	Miserable (IV)	Anxious (I)

ATTITUDE

Ironically the same thing can happen when:

- An employee has reached the top of his or her current job-cycle and has moved into the bored/frustrated quadrant. They start looking for another job and in order to hold onto them the organisation offers them a "coercive promotion" or otherwise moves them into a post for which they are simply not prepared.

- A skilled employee who is particularly good at his or her job is promoted into a management position.

Here again, the root of the problem is the manner in which organisations recruit, because recruiting focuses on what people have *already* done rather than what they might be capable of doing. This attitude compounds the proclivity to recruit people at the top of the "doom loop" in the manner described earlier.

I experienced this myself recently when seeking some guidance in updating my CV. After some years of really struggling to come up with a document that conveyed the essence of who I am and what I am about, I thought I had finally succeeded. To make sure that this wasn't just self-delusion on my part, I sent a copy to a friend in advertising and to another who is a specialist head-hunter, and both seemed to think I was onto a winner. I then presented the results of my efforts to my mentor who told me that I had it back to front and the "appendix" that I had added to describe the companies I had worked for and the roles that I had filled with them was the most important part and the section that employers were most interested in. As his line of business is recruitment, I have no doubt that he is an expert and therefore right. However, I have to question the practice on which his guidance is based.

Imagine for the moment that you are supreme commander of a national army, preparing for battle with a rather daunting enemy. A messenger arrives from the enemy forces offering you the opportunity to avoid all the bloodshed associated with a full-scale battle but instead decide the outcome on a winner-takes-all basis determined by a single one-on-one combat between your best soldier and their best soldier. The offer strikes you as being a bit like having a penalty shoot-out without first playing the match, but is nevertheless tempting and so you agree. You then discover that their champion is a giant 9 feet 4 inches tall and that he is (hardly surprisingly) undefeated throughout his career. Your current champion takes one look at the man and immediately retires from all international competition.

Now you are in a bit of a pickle. You are already committed to the match but there is no immediate successor and in any case every potential candidate has either remembered that they have a previous engagement or else has had to rush back home to attend their grandmother's funeral. You are obliged to advertise, but only one candidate responds. He is a healthy looking lad with red hair but his only career experience is as a shepherd boy. If the situation wasn't so serious you might even laugh. Nevertheless your equal opportunities programme prevents you from discriminating against shepherds and you duly interview the lad. During the interview you ask him why on earth he thinks he can do the job and he tells you that while protecting his father's sheep he has single-handedly killed a lion and a bear. You point out that this is very encouraging but is not quite the same as armed combat and particularly armed combat with an experienced soldier who happens to be considerably bigger than a bear.

Against all better judgement, but coloured largely by the fact that you have no other choice, you agree to appoint the lad as your champion. You get your Quartermaster General to organise a fresh suit of armour for him and to find a nice sharp sword for him from the armoury. You are amazed, however, when the lad tries them out but decides that they are too heavy and restrict his movement, as well as making him sweat too much, and so refuses to use them. At this stage you see a life of slavery looming before you, but you have to concede that there is no point in sending him out to fight with equipment that he has never used anyway, and you try to put on a brave face as he goes forward intrepidly with his stones and slingshot to meet the enemy champion.

Of course you will have recognised this as a loose rendition of the story of David and Goliath. Now this may be considered rather an extreme example, for there was no-one who had the experience of taking on a champion like Goliath, and David appeared to be the only one who was willing to do so, in which case they really didn't have much choice. Even then, after accepting David as their champion, they still tried to dictate how he should fight and attempted to kit him out in armour to fight in the manner expected. However, David was the ultimate "I do it Daddy!" child and, because of his trust in his god and his past experience, and certainty that he would be sustained, he was justifiably confident that he could meet the challenge.

The fact remains, however, that both the challenge and the circumstances were new to David and he had no experience of the armed combat that the job apparently called for. His CV highlighted the fact he was a shepherd boy with no military experience whatsoever. Only when interviewed was he able to recount the examples of his courage and strength and convince others of his potential for the role. And that is my concern with the presentation of CVs that emphasise what roles one played and in what organisation. This is because they:

- Focus on the role rather than the person filling the position.
- Are rooted in a mindset that expects a person to keep on doing much the same thing.
- Tend to look at the past as an indicator of potential rather than the person as a whole.
- Completely ignore aspirations. It is an approach that would normally have rejected David entirely and limited his career prospects to that of being a shepherd or possibly a farmer for the rest of his life.

Consequently, when at last I had identified a way to build my achievements into my CV in a way that *in my opinion* gives a reader a better sense of what I have done, what is important to me and, most significantly, my potential in different situations, and am being told that this is only important in connection with where I did it and my job title then, I have to ask, "Is it really me that is back to front?"

Initially, I thought perhaps it was. After all, the sheer weight of numbers says it has to be. But recently I came across the following case study which seems to provide empirical evidence for my way of thinking.[1]

---

[1] The following case was developed by Andrew O'Connell of Omni HR Solutions (UK) and has been extracted almost verbatim from the Onrec.com website with his permission.

The Challenge

It was 1990 and BP and the Australian Commonwealth Employment service (CES) had a problem. They were jointly running a scheme to provide long term unemployed teenagers with jobs as forecourt attendants. The government was providing customer service training followed by 3 months subsidised salary, whilst BP was providing full time jobs for successful trainees. However, only 1 in 5 trainees were still in employment at the end of the three months.

With training and subsidies approaching $20,000 per head the future of the entire program was at risk. Results from schemes with other employers were equally poor – so it was unlikely that the high attrition rate could be attributed to BP or the job itself. The problem seemed to be far too many candidates being placed on the program who were unsuitable for customer service roles.

To ensure that the scheme was continued it was imperative that the retention rate was increased. BP was unlikely to retain interest while the quality of the potential employees remained low and there was little benefit to the long term unemployed teenagers to be trained for a job in which they had no interest.

The objectives were to increase employee retention, improve the overall quality of the candidates and to provide the teenagers with jobs they would be happy and successful at.

What makes a good forecourt attendant?

To start with, BP/CES needed to establish if there were any personal characteristics that indicated whether someone would be a first-class customer service representative. One in 5 of the teenagers who had started the course were successful. Was there a pattern to aspects of their personality that were different from the 4 in 5 who didn't complete the program?

If there were differences then teenagers could be 'cast' into customer service roles, as a director 'casts' actors in a play. Many people could play Romeo, but only actors with certain characteristics are suited to playing the great lover successfully.

At this point BP/CES approached Harrison Assessments (HA) who had developed a profiling system which measured a large number of behavioural tendencies, interests and preferences. The system, which was called InnerView, was based on 2 main theories.

Enjoyment-Performance Theory which states that if an individual enjoys performing a certain task or behaving in a particular way, they will act in that way more frequently and these particular traits will, as a result, become better developed. The converse applies to those behaviours and tasks we don't enjoy.

Psycho-Paradox Theory is more complicated, but essentially states that apparently contradictory, or mutually exclusive traits, (e.g. diplomacy and frankness), are in fact complementary. InnerView doesn't simply measure whether an individual is more diplomatic or more frank, but measures both traits independently. An individual who is both very frank and very diplomatic will be a far better communicator than someone who is neither.

HA examined 130 behavioural traits from a number of previously successful and unsuccessful forecourt attendants. The results did indeed show that there were a number of characteristics that would indicate a 'winner' at customer service in the forecourt environment.

Just as a casting director will be looking for sensitive eyes and a lithe grace for his Romeo, star customer service staff have the following traits:

- Warmth/Empathy
- Diplomacy
- Outgoingness (extroversion)
- Helpfulness
- Tolerance of Bluntness (tolerance of customers who are rude or blunt)
- Cooperativeness
- Organised
- Self-Motivation

In addition, the following traits were found to be counter productive:

- Rebelliousness
- Bluntness
- Dogmatism
- Harshness (excessive strictness)

TRAINING FOR SERVICE

Just as a suitable actor couldn't play Romeo without preparation, rehearsal and direction – customer service staff also required proper training and experience before they can be successful.

So, armed with the new pre-screening system a panel of BP and CES staff interviewed teenage applicants for the forecourt attendant training scheme. None of the applicants were guaranteed a job if they got a place on the course but they clearly had an advantage if they did well.

Many of the panel however, were experienced recruiters and they were sceptical of the pre-screening system. Although given the results of the screening before the interview, they still accepted several teenagers that the system indicated did not have the right level and mix of characteristics to succeed. The screening, however, was proved to be correct and the teenagers deemed to be unsuitable for customer service began to seriously disrupt the course.

This led the panel to rethink the use of the system on subsequent courses and only those candidates who were both suitable for customer service and did well in the interview were accepted for training. It is important to remember that the screening was an adjunct to the recruitment process, not a replacement for the face to face interaction.

THE JOB

On successfully completing the course the trainees were invited to apply for a role as a BP forecourt attendant. There was no compulsion for them to do so. During the first three months BP conducted mystery shopping research at their service stations to gauge the level of 'customer experience' the graduates were providing. The results were very pleasing

THE RESULTS

Overall, 601 long-term unemployed teenagers applied for the BP/CES scheme. 94 made it through the screening and interview process to begin training and 95% of the applicants predicted to succeed completed the course successfully. The results also showed that 4 of the 6 applicants rated as "unsuitable" failed to complete the course.

By the end of the three-month period the number of previously long term unemployed teenagers still in the job had risen from 19% to 83%. These same teenagers were achieving customer service ratings (from mystery shopper surveys) 15% higher than the national average. In addition, stores with these teenagers reported sales increases of up to 25% on some product lines.

As far as the CES were concerned the savings in training costs realised by selecting only people who are suitable for customer service was over $1,000,000 across the 5 courses.

THE LESSONS

Customer service is the face any organisation presents to the world and how an organisation interacts with its customers can define the organisation itself. Dealing with people who are genuinely warm and helpful is enjoyable for the customer. All of us can play a number of roles in life and simply by screening for candidates who were suitable for this particular role, BP made an enormous positive difference to their profits, their customer experience and a to large group of previously unemployed teenagers.

***

If we are to value people properly and treat them as assets our approach has to change. The optimum relationship between employer and employee will only happen when the mutual dependence is fully understood and appreciated.

Employees who are achieving personal fulfilment and constantly pushing the boundaries of their personal capability will contribute the most to the organisation and it is in both party's interests to strive to that end. That means starting with the whole person and not just a job-filler.

IS THERE A MODEL FOR THIS?

Perhaps professional team sport is the closest example there is to the ideal. Players are "bought" in the market place and developed to fulfil their own expectations and/or those of their employer. If they succeed, their value in the marketplace increases and they move on to bigger roles in bigger teams or else they are traded or sold to lesser teams where there is a better match with their capabilities. Similarly, as they get older and their abilities wane, they retire or move down the ranks or into areas requiring different skills but calling upon the benefit of their experience.

So, clearly, the industry can be said to have pioneered the concept of people as assets, for players that cost millions are certainly reflected in the books. Thus, it would seem that the principles adopted in the sports industry could be used as a basis for the wider commercial field at large. Let us explore some of the possibilities.

ACCOUNTING FOR PEOPLE

Cost of Acquisition

It might not be on anything like the same scale as sports stars, but most employees do have a cost of acquisition. While sports stars may have a purchase price that includes a hefty agent's commission, even the lowest level clerical worker usually comes with an "agent's fee" represented by the proportion of their starting salary that is paid to the recruitment consultancy responsible for the "placement". Even where the entire search and selection process is handled in-house, there is a cost associated with the time, effort and overhead of the recruitment. I therefore recommend that, as a first step in recognising and treating employees as assets, these recruitment costs should be capitalised and appear in the balance sheet as an asset. Not only would this start to bring home the message that people are indeed assets, but it would also highlight the "cost" of staff turnover in a manner that would bring home the lessons that current performance measures fail to do.

In instances where recruitment is done informally, e.g. through personal introduction and recommendation, and there is little or no directly attributable cost, a notional cost should be recorded, equivalent to the cost that would have been incurred if the normal channels had been pursued.

Appreciation

As mentioned earlier, unlike normal "capital" assets, human assets are more likely to appreciate than depreciate. Thus, if they are going to be valued in the books, a method needs to be found for handling this. There are a number of possibilities for this and any one or more of the following are recommended as starting points:

1. The cost or a "reasonable" (fixed and justified) proportion of any training undertaken should be added to the employee's asset value. This would offer a number of benefits:

- It would mean that training was no longer an expense, hidden in the non-disclosed section of the financial statements. Stakeholders would be able to assess the extent to which businesses are prepared to "invest" in their human resources.

- No longer regarding training as an expense means that it would no longer be one of the first elements to be considered for reduction during downturns in the business.

- The higher visibility of training and personal development would mean that greater thought was given to the type of training offered.

- Both parties would be more committed to the whole concept and all it entails.
- It would encourage greater effort to see that the benefits from the training were realised in the day-to-day work.

2. Every time an employee is promoted, their acquisition cost should be adjusted by a fixed percentage, broadly enough to recognise the additional outlay that would be incurred if the person were to be recruited for the new position.

3. Every time a person earns an award or is given a pay-increase over and above the "going rate" in order to recognise their contribution, this should be factored into their value, because it recognises that they are committed to a higher level of performance and therefore should be retained.

Depreciation

While it is to be expected that recognising and accounting for employees as assets in this way would revolutionise the workplace and boost motivation and productivity, there may be times when their value may diminish and this needs to be recognised and accounted for as well.

While this is readily acceptable for a sports star suffering injury or whose performance dips, it needs to be understood that the same thing can happen to regular workers. Whether for health reasons, problems outside of the work environment, or simply because specialist skills have become redundant in the face of new technology and processes, people's value may diminish. Recognising this and adjusting for it accordingly by reducing the value at which they are held in the books will:

- Ensure that the human capital is fairly valued in the books rather than being consistently overvalued.
- Reinforce the motivational aspects of the whole valuation principle as any decline in value may reflect badly on the employee concerned.

Some might argue that this could have a negative effect and possibly discourage employees further, creating a downward spiral. The risk of this would be minimal because nobody ever sets out to do a poor job and, if handled properly, the identification of a negative trend should be seen as a positive reinforcement for modified behaviour and that, after all, is the objective. If it does not have that effect and the downward tendency continues or accelerates, it is simply empirical evidence that the asset has declining value and needs to be traded or sold.

Ownership

Of course there is one major difference between "people" and other capital assets. The latter are "owned" by the company. They have been acquired with all the rights of vested "ownership" that allows the company to use them in virtually any manner in which they see fit. This is not the case with employees, which is why the employment contract is one of "hire" as alluded to earlier.

The question of "ownership" of people is an emotive issue. Apart from the historic precedent of slavery, modern Western civil liberties make the concept a complete anathema. However, it is a subject that needs to be objectively analysed, for the line is a very fine one and in fact rather blurred.

When a business has invested the massive sums in a sports star, it could be said to "own" that star. It has greater control than most employers over the personal "rights" of the individual that may go so far as to determine how they will conduct themselves in private and even when they can or cannot have sex! The organisational objectives are paramount and the "persona" of the star has to develop within the parameters set by those boundaries. Any attempt to move beyond those and become "bigger than the organisation" is met with brutal power.

One simply has to look at David Beckham's departure from Manchester United for an example of this. In the light of his commercial value to the club, Beckham's "sale" to Real Madrid was a virtual giveaway. He probably recovered the price paid for him by Real Madrid in terms of publicity and product sales within months! So why did Manchester United let him go? Most likely because his personal profile was considered to be undermining the ethos of the club and there was a fear that his outside interests were taking his attention away from football.

While such "ownership" may be considered extreme, is it so very different from any other business environment? Enron is a modern classic of how the corporate culture took over the lives and the values of its employees. The fact is that all too often our employment contracts and the fear of their loss dominates lives and governs behaviour. So where is the line that defines "ownership"?

Perhaps employment law is already a de facto alternative form of "ownership". However, it is an issue that needs further consideration in the context of valuing employees as assets.

Disposal

The question of "ownership" is particularly pertinent when it comes to dispensing with human assets that are no longer deemed appropriate. From an accounting perspective this would be no different to disposing of any other "fixed asset" with the profit or loss on disposal being accounted for at the time.

While football has its "Bosman rules" and other sports their own rules that dictate when a star can become a "free agent", this concept is new to "normal" business and may put a whole new wrinkle on the labour market.

Conclusion

Treating employees as human assets and valuing them accordingly, along the lines suggested, would be a win-win for both employers and employees. It would reinforce positive behaviour by both parties through both the positive and negative reinforcement tools inherent in the practice. There may be legal issues of "ownership" that need to be resolved and formalised, but generally the accounting treatment would broadly follow the precedent of fixed assets, with the only major difference being the need to recognise and record asset appreciation as well as depreciation. However, efforts to do so would remove some of the anomalies and distortions that result from current accounting practices and the simple expensing of employee-related costs.

More than anything though, treating people as assets, recruiting them as such (as is frequently done in graduate recruitment programmes), and accounting for them in the same way, would align personal objectives with those of the organisation, create more aware employees who are motivated to take responsibility for their own working lives, and thus go a long way towards resolving the industrial conflict that has existed between management and their workers throughout the industrial age.

Treating people as assets will create greater employee/employer awareness and induce greater organisational alignment – and thus ensure a triple A organisation!

Lean Organisations Need FAT People

CHAPTER 7

TIME TO "'T' ON"

"You cannot offer good service through a set of rigid rules"
John Timpson: Chairman & CEO, Timpson Limited[1]

A new employer/employee alignment based on optimising personal development with a view to fulfilling personal potential, and a new system of accounting for employees as assets, will radically alter the "master-servant" relationship that underpins current employment law and practice. It is therefore not something that will happen overnight and needs to be thought through from every angle.

The biggest issue is unquestionably likely to be one of cost. Regardless of the nature of an organisation there is always a bottom line focus, which obviously necessitates keeping outlays to a minimum. Thus, I can already hear the protestations from employers, "It's all very well, but what is it going to add to our employment costs? We cannot possibly think of going down that road – it'll be too costly!"

In an economy facing enormous pension deficits and increased national insurance costs, this is a very understandable response, and employers will rightly be wary. This is, however, a knee-jerk reaction predicated on "employees as costs" thinking, which is precisely the mentality being challenged. So let's dig a little deeper.

---

[1] Timpson Limited is noteworthy for featuring prominently in The Sunday Times "100 Best Companies To Work For" every year in the decade or so since its inception, with ranking based on employee feedback – the result of their recognition and appreciation of the lengths to which the company goes to let staff make their own decisions. The company proves my point that empowered people provide better service and hence increased profits.

THE COMMERCIAL EDGE

The effectiveness of any organisation ultimately boils down to its people. If two businesses are manufacturing widgets, they will require premises and equipment with which to do so. Assuming that there are no capital constraints (and in a market where there are effectively no constraints on acquiring capital providing there is a sound business case, this is not an unrealistic assumption) each will have state of the art equipment with comparable productive capability. Consequently any difference in performance has to be attributable to the people and the processes that they develop and oversee.

Thus, there can be no getting away from the fact that people really are an organisation's greatest asset

PEOPLE AND PROFIT

The implications of the foregoing are profound for, if people are the major differentiators between organisations, then it follows logically that the degree of profit is directly attributable to the human endeavour.

This is hardly a new idea. Yet, for the entire Industrial Age, capitalist theory has taught that profit is the reward for risk, earned by the investor in the business. While this could be justified historically on the grounds that capital was a scarce resource while labour was generally freely available, the case is not so clear-cut in the Information Age, when the reverse is truer, with capital no longer scarce and the labour market considerably more complex. It is therefore time to challenge the conventional wisdom and reconsider the underlying theories.

As we saw earlier, the biggest change in organisational dynamics in the Information Age has been the devolution of power. In an Internet age, where responses are demanded almost instantly, delays can threaten the very survival of the business. Such a fast-paced, competitive world means decisions can no longer be the sole prerogative of managers with greater expertise or experience, but have to move down the "command chain". At the same time, wrong decisions are not only costly but can be equally disastrous. This inevitably means that greater responsibility than ever before is being delegated to employees, who can individually impact on the results of the organisation as a whole.

In such an environment, organisational failure can stem just as easily from the shortcomings of a junior employee as it could from the incorrect strategy adopted by a senior employee such as the CEO.

So, clearly, it is in the organisation's best interest to ensure that every employee is progressing individually and not falling back into a doom loop. Not only will such people be less prone to making mistakes but, because they are challenged and stimulated, they will inevitably be more productive than those who are not and the results will be reflected in the organisation's effectiveness – and its profits.

Operating the kind of personal development partnership that we have been contemplating is going to be essential for future success. The successful organisation of the 21st century is going to be the one in which:

- Personal development is accepted employment practice for all employees, with proper alignment between personal objectives and organisational needs.
- Effective organisational teamwork is a primary goal.

THE FIFTH COLUMN

This has been recognised and addressed in such things as knowledge management, the learning organisation, and continuous improvement programmes. It is also implicitly recognised in the trend towards flatter organisations. However, these are only partial solutions and the full implications have been recognised by very few organisations, if any. If you doubt this, just ask yourself how many organisations you know that, despite proud boasts that people are their greatest assets, attribute their success to their people, and make a practical link between their people and their profits or performance?

Business Week (April 9, 2001) reported that in the US, "CEO pay has sky-rocketed by 434% since 1991, while the average worker's pay rose by 34%." It went on that; "In 2000, the average CEO salary was 531 times that of the blue collar worker." Indications are that the trend is similar in the UK and elsewhere. What more evidence do you need that this fundamental principle of the value of people has not yet been understood? In an era where organisational teamwork is critical to success, the very bonds of teamwork are undermined by those responsible for developing and promoting it!

Unfortunately I don't have the statistics to prove it, but I would be willing to bet, based on my own experience and observation, that in a large proportion of those companies where CEO pay had risen so astronomically, there had also been some sort of corporate headcount reduction programme.

Common sense says that this kind of disparity cannot continue. If employee numbers continue to fall and the gap between rich and poor becomes visibly greater, it will inevitably lead to an increasingly militant work force with a surge in trade union belligerence. Indeed, there are signs that this is already happening. That it should come to that is an indictment on executive management, as it makes it perfectly clear that they have not understood the changing dynamics of the workplace and are effectively sabotaging their own organisations by destroying any possibility of the type of teamwork necessary for modern business.

DEMOCRACY VS. TEAMWORK

Effective organisational teamwork is key to long-term organisational success. In simple terms this requires:

- A universal commitment to a shared vision.

- Every member to know their role and what is expected of them.

- Every member to strive continually to improve their personal performance and meet and exceed expectations.

- Members to support one another to the best of their ability, including stepping into another's role temporarily should the need arise.

- Effortless and effective communication.

- Authority vested in key members who have a recognised and accepted role in decision making and/or the handling of conflict, should there be any.

- Problems being quickly identified and appropriate corrective action agreed and taken.

There is nothing in this that stipulates that every member has to have equal standing or be equally rewarded, but there is an implicit recognition of and respect for the skills and abilities that each person brings, as well as their right to freely express an opinion about anything to do with the team's objectives and operation. Teamwork and democracy are by no means synonymous!

Nevertheless, as we have already seen, wildly disparate remuneration is unlikely to build a good team ethic and thus the whole question of remuneration is pivotal to organisational effectiveness.

THE INVASION OF PERFORMANCE RELATED PAY

The idea of paying for results is hardly a new one. Piecework is a tradition as old as commerce itself. Yet, notwithstanding that, Performance Related Pay (PRP) or Incentive Based Remuneration (IBR) has hardly been a standard feature of Industrial Age reward. Entrepreneurs have preferred to maximise profits by attempting to keep wages and salaries as a fixed cost rather than a variable one, and linking pay to performance has generally been limited to either the agricultural industries, where it was already prevalent, or to sales commissions.

With the increasing segregation between the owners and the professional managers appointed to run the business, however, another type of PRP developed – the bonus. Initially confined to the most senior levels of management, bonuses were intended to encourage management to think more like owners and historically were often simply dependent on a profit being made rather than being tied to specific performance results.

Yet, in the past decade or two this has changed. Starting with the concept of Managing By Objectives (MBO), which tied rewards to the achievement of more specific objectives, it was soon recognised that the bonus model could be applied more universally. So, it therefore evolved from being a fashionable executive remuneration tool into something much more definitive. Trickling down the organisation, the bonus initially was used to shape and reward desired behaviour at all levels of management, but it rapidly spread further, becoming a key implement in the organisational development toolbox, being used to mould nearly all employee behaviour and to focus their efforts more definitely.

The degree to which PRP has become integral to almost all employees' income is quite amazing. Look at any employment advertising today and you will see that the large majority offer

"OTE" (On Target Earnings), indicating bonuses are pervasive and any position that does not offer a bonus is the exception rather than the norm. Yet I can remember in the early eighties thinking that it was not fair that salespeople had the ability to increase their incomes almost infinitely, whilst I could work longer hours and put in an equivalent effort or more and yet receive no tangible benefit whatsoever. Now everyone has them. The practice has even spread to the civil service!

So, in little more than a decade the concept has moved from theory to conventional wisdom. Is this, however, the panacea that it is believed to be?

The concept has definitely been a step in the right direction and a vast improvement on what existed before. There is also a considerable danger that – as with most trends – it has become fashionable and thus in many instances unlikely to have been properly thought through and implemented. We have already seen that incentives only have a short-term effect, and so the likelihood is that, after initial productivity gains, they will lose their effectiveness; something I doubt has been factored into most organisational schemes.

Performance Measurement

With Incentive Pay becoming general practice it is perhaps inevitable that there has been corresponding attention to the issue of performance measurement – after all, it is part of the equation.

Inevitably, however, the link back to the bottom line has meant that ways have to be found to tie individual performance to corporate performance. While this is obviously desirable, it has also proved to be a two-edged sword as executive management has been forced to chase a stream of never-ending improvement in order to justify their own incentive remuneration – likely a contributory factor in the recent epidemic of false accounting.

The extent and speed of this pervasiveness in current corporate strategy is perhaps best illustrated by Robert Eccles in his article "The Performance Measurement Manifesto" (Harvard Business Review, January-February 1991.) He maintains: *"More and more managers are changing their company's performance measurement systems to track non-financial measures and reinforce competitive strategies"*. And he lists as one of five essential activities, "aligning bonuses and other incentives with the new system".

INCENTIVES AND STRATEGY

This gives a clear indication of a broadening of the role of PRP. It provides a classic example of what any project manager would recognise as "scope-creep", for not only has the scale of the concept spread, but also the objective. As it becomes tied in to reinforcing strategy – and particularly "new competitive strategies" – it switches from being an operational tool, facilitating the effective contribution of employees to their defined roles, to being a change agent compelling dynamic shifts in behaviour.

It is debatable whether any tool can be realistically expected to address the different requirements of operational, tactical and strategic management simultaneously. PRP may be a "miracle cure" that does offer the possibility, but the inherent dangers of attempting to use it in this way need to be identified and addressed.

Most obvious is the divide between the present and the envisioned strategy. Like the swimming duck, where there is no obvious sign of activity on the surface but considerable effort expended below the surface to control both movement and direction, to remain in business any organisation relies on the effective execution of the mundane and repetitive activities resulting from daily transactions. Removing the measures that focus on these activities is to risk chaos.

Perhaps the single biggest challenge facing executives today is the need to create organisations that are responsive to change and able to react quickly to new strategies necessitated by the pressures of modern competition. It is therefore hardly surprising that there is a temptation to use PRP as the way to address this, but – like most temptation – it is better resisted.

Hopefully, the employer/employee collaboration I am promoting will be acknowledged to offer a better alternative.

DRAWBACKS OF INCENTIVE BASED REMUNERATION

While the theory behind PRP is unquestionably sound, there are a number of practical shortcomings that detract from its effectiveness.

Basis of Reward

One of the primary issues is the nature of the incentive payment itself. Most, if not all, incentive schemes contain inherent deficiencies which are either unrecognised or disregarded by management when the scheme is implemented, whether wilfully, or simply because no better alternative solution has been conceived. This can be illustrated by looking at the most prevalent types of incentive schemes that are used.

Personal Bonuses

Bonuses paid on the basis of individual performance may not necessarily be equitable. Managers may (like teachers) have "pets" – staff with whom they identify more than others and whom they might sub-consciously favour. Even if they don't, or are able to conceal their preferences, their actions may still be subject to interpretation and challenged.

Whether the fact is recognised or not, bonuses inevitably bring us back into the arena of effort and perception that we discussed earlier, and consequently there may be an unavoidable subjectivity in their award, not only according to the style of the manager who determines the performance levels, but also because Employee A may need to do perceivably less to "justify" their bonus than Employee B. Over time this can, and probably will, cause dissatisfaction.

Team Bonuses

Bonuses paid on the basis of team performance can suffer from the same problems, albeit on perhaps a slightly larger scale. While such bonuses may encourage an environment in which peer pressure becomes an additional factor in shaping desired behaviour, and thus encourages greater effort from those who might not otherwise exert themselves in their working environment, they can also create a competitive environment whereby teams actively pursuing their own team objectives may deliberately or inadvertently prevent others from achieving theirs. I have worked in companies where this has happened, and the conflict has ultimately been counterproductive to the organisation as a whole.

Furthermore, they can also discourage personal effort and be totally demotivating. For instance, for a previous employer, because of the amount of unpaid overtime I worked, I personally generated between one-and-a-half and two times my annual salary in additional revenue for work that was acclaimed by the ultimate client. Yet, because the team had failed to meet its overall revenue targets, I received no reward or recognition whatsoever for my effort. There were no performance bonuses, and to make matters worse, pay increases were frozen and nobody even acknowledged the contribution that I had made. And employers wonder why they cannot get loyal service from their employees!

Share Options

These are usually restricted to listed companies whose shares are traded, but they can also be offered by start-up or growing smaller companies with big ambitions and high hopes. In either case, they tend to be favoured by more entrepreneurial managers or organisations that want to engender a more entrepreneurial culture. However, they will only work as long as the share price is climbing. The minute the share price falls they lose all their motivational powers.

Very attractive to developing companies that are expected to grow and thus anticipate a steadily rising share price, share options provide a means of rewarding employees with no real cash cost and hence no negative impact on the Profit & Loss Account.

While this offers a potential win-win for all, lower-paid employees can be at a disadvantage because of a lack of financial sophistication and/or the lack of financial resources with which to afford them. Even if they do appreciate them, their primary need is for cash and so they will be more likely to simply buy and sell simultaneously. Consequently the intention of making them more committed to the company and to "think like share-holders" is largely mitigated.

However, perhaps the biggest drawback to share-options is the part they play in creating a two-tier reward system, whereby management, particularly executive management, are able to achieve significantly bigger earnings. Share options offer a very effective means of circumventing the traditional salary bands associated with grades, and have all too often been abused. In organisations where teamwork is paramount, openness and integrity are essential and share options are hardly conducive.

Shares

These can be offered in any company but usually tend to fall into two categories:

- Very small companies where individuals play a major part in their development.

- Listed companies where shares are traded and their award has a negligible impact on the distribution of power.

These can be very dangerous in their consequences for small companies if and when there is any change in any of the owners' circumstances. Not only are they difficult to value, but they need a very strong (and costly) legal arrangement to ensure that the original company objectives can be pursued without any loss of direction or focus. Many a successful company has folded as a result of a founding shareholder's inability to regain control of the company that he or she started.

For listed companies, the intention behind share offerings is to encourage employees to think like owners and thus to help develop a sense of common purpose and an innate team ethic, hopefully whilst also encouraging a more long-term perspective. However, while the theory is good the outcome is invariably somewhat different because:

- Once again the lower paid employees need cash and so simply dispose of any shares they are awarded.

- Being paid in shares is fundamentally inconvenient.
- The final value received may not be consistent with the promise received, thus the motivational benefits may be diluted or lost.

In any event, it is only the senior personnel who can relate the value of shares to their actions and consequently the link to aligned long-term thinking becomes tenuous. Even then, it is questionable whether a focus on share price is not to the ultimate detriment of the long-term good of the company – an issue that we will shortly explore in greater detail.

I have experienced the negatives first hand. Whilst working for a major international American company, we employees were told – with no discussion – that henceforth all bonuses would be paid in shares. The justification for this scheme was that:

- By only taking possession of the shares after three years we could avoid paying income tax on them.
- The value of the shares would increase over that time, giving us a further benefit considerably greater than we would get from a cash payment.
- There would be even greater rewards from long term ownership.
- We would all have a greater affinity with the operation of the company and hence be more committed.

The company really tried to convey the fact that the decision was taken in employees' best interests and that we could only benefit. Of course the reality was quite different! This was because:

1. The shares decreased in value – quite considerably. In one instance, shares that were awarded at a price of more than $37 were worth less than a third of that by the time they actually vested.

2. The dollar decreased significantly in value against the pound, creating a double-whammy.

The effect of this was to completely nullify the supposed advantage of the tax break. Perhaps this is just an unfortunate example, but the fact remains that it not only created a risk that employees were never even given an option to accept or reject, but the autocratic manner in which it was implemented also defeated the primary purpose underpinning the scheme, and instead of creating greater goodwill within the organisation, it simply created resentment and a feeling of having been ripped off. The high-handed approach immediately nullified the intended effects of the decision from the start, and simply created resentment over the ultimate message conveyed, which was that the organisation's interests took precedence over those of its employees.

Profit Sharing

This is perhaps the most obvious alternative to any of the schemes outlined, and one that is becoming increasingly popular. In my opinion it is also the best. However, even this has inherent drawbacks.

Firstly, the proportion of profit to be shared needs to be defined and consistent. It is not something that can be left to the arbitrary decision of management.

Secondly, the basis of sharing has to be open, fair and equitable. The type of situation in which executives receive 100% of their salaries while lower graded staff receive 2-5% is hardly likely to achieve the kind of corporate teamwork and dedication that is desirable.

There is a further issue with profit sharing that I believe has to be taken into account, namely that if people are to be rewarded on the basis of profit their contribution towards it has to be recognised as well as their ability to influence factors which affect it. Remember, we are talking here about creating corporate teamwork where people can not only make decisions when they need to, but are willing and able to step up to the plate when the occasion arises, in precisely the way Timpson has done.

My thoughts on this are coloured by my own experience in a situation in which increased divisional profitability was one of the stated criteria for me to earn my bonus. I refused to accept this, explaining to my manager that the scope of my role meant I had no direct control over this. His succinct response was, "It is one of my measures and everyone in my team shares it, otherwise they cannot be part of my team". I decided to go along with that, not only as I did not want to lose my job, but also because I felt that several years of double-digit profit growth were indicative of management's strategic commitment to that objective and therefore accepting it would simply mean that I could focus more attention on my other performance measures. After all, if we didn't make a profit there would be no bonuses anyway.

Well, guess what? That's the way it turned out! The division and the company made its first loss in 90 years and I shall never forget the corporate despair and the negative effect on motivation and morale of the realisation that there was absolutely nothing that could be done to generate earnings that were taken for granted and on which lifestyles revolved. The problem with most incentive schemes is that they are rooted in optimism and seldom look at worst-case scenarios – a flaw which makes them dangerous in bad times. Then they somehow tend to be far more effective at reinforcing negative behaviour than they ever are at reinforcing positive behaviour during the good times.

Ubiquity

The growth of PRP in the past decade or so has transcended fashion to the extent that it has become almost ubiquitous. While not inherently a bad thing, the unfortunate consequence of this is that it is often not properly implemented. Too often, the incentive element is factored into the total package offered, with the result that the incentive element is effectively lost and the scheme becomes counterproductive because:

- It becomes a kind of enforced savings program for employees with payment amounting to little more than an additional salary payment.

- The base salary then becomes less than the "going rate" making the employee feel exploited.

- In the event of non-payment the employee becomes demoralised and de-motivated.

Limited Employee Control of Factors Affecting Entitlement

The objective of any incentive is to encourage the employee to work harder or produce more than they otherwise might. It is thus vital for any effective incentive that the performance measured is tied exclusively to elements over which the employee has some control. This is often more difficult than it would seem. It is not without reason that incentive based remuneration was not an integral part of industrial age production from the word go. For, while an apple picker could exercise some control over what was picked – the quality, the time spent picking, when to pick, etc. – the productivity of factory workers was more dependent on organisational factors beyond their personal control.

A consulting organisation had introduced an incentive scheme whereby bonuses were paid to consultants based on the overall utilisation of consultants within their respective skill-sets or teams. This was generally considered a success, but then the company unilaterally changed the base to personal utilisation. As consultants had no control over the marketing of their services and thus the hours they were able to bill, this was seen as a way for the company to effectively reduce their earnings and consequently had a serious effect on morale and, ultimately, staff turnover. Such unilateralism is not uncommon, but an incentive developed without the input of those being measured is hardly worth the name and is unlikely to be successful.

Lack of Mutual Development

It is therefore essential for effective incentives that both employees and employers are party to the development of the scheme. While developing employee performance measures clearly needs to be done in conjunction with employees, it is just as important that the employee understands the company's position and what constitutes effective performance and why. Both parties need to understand the factors that are likely to affect performance and their consequences and factor these into both assessing the performance measures and the remuneration warranted.

It is all too easy for either one or both parties to become dissatisfied when the conditions have not been clearly agreed initially. However, it is unlikely that all possible conditions and eventualities will be covered in every scheme. Consequently, it is even more important that the scheme is developed in a spirit of co-operation and mutual trust, so that reasonable compromises can be developed in the event of unforeseen circumstances.

This implies not only a large degree of initial cooperation, but also ongoing collaboration to refine the "rules" and ensure that circumstances governing performance are properly evaluated. One has to question how often this happens in the "real world" and thus the extent to which incentives are truly justified.

Divisive Rather Than Uniting Force

Increasingly, the consequences of incentive schemes appear to be a focus on meeting the criteria that determine whether or not incremental payment is forthcoming. Rather than fostering team effort and organisational co-operation and goodwill, this can erode it. While the theory is that the achievement of the goal is good for the organisation, the single-mindedness with which it is pursued can cause problems elsewhere.

For example, a financial services company had a strategy whereby all administrative costs were cross-charged to the revenue generating departments and every such department was regarded as a profit centre in its own right, with its own profit and loss statement. The management of each of these "businesses" was expected to generate bottom line growth of not less than 15% and had bonuses of 10-40% of their gross remuneration riding on the achievement of such profits. Obviously this created internal conflict, but the executive management team actively encouraged this, believing it encouraged entrepreneurial thinking and thereby forced managers to act as if they owned the business.

The results of this strategy were:

- Firstly, the conflict inevitably extended to the administrative areas. Not only were they expected to keep their charges to a minimum (below those that could be obtained externally), but they were constantly caught up justifying their charges and their allocations, with the result that more time was spent looking inwards than on meeting customer needs. As a result, service declined, complaints rose, and customers ultimately took their business elsewhere.

- Secondly, sales staff earned commission for "new business" by each "business category", resulting in commissions payments even when funds were transferred from one type of account to another. Market forces at that time favoured investment in mutual funds and so this division experienced record growth, even though this was merely the result of churned funds from money already held on deposit. As a consequence, commissions were paid when there was no additional benefit for the organisation and the mutual funds team were substantially rewarded for meeting their objectives while the retail funds team received no bonuses at all.

During the first year or two it proved relatively easy to achieve 15% growth, particularly as the economy was booming. However, such growth targets became unreasonable. Yet there was no flexibility and the 15% remained fixed, even though managers had no powers to make the kind of strategic innovation that might have allowed it. Aggravated by a downturn in the economy, the situation was made even worse by the friction resulting from managers desperately trying to safeguard their positions.

As a result the company, inevitably, did not survive in its existing shape, but was taken over by a rival organisation. While this may be an extreme case, it highlights the pitfalls that can arise from not aligning objectives properly, and it is by no means unique.

Incentives, as intended, will always govern behaviour. Conflict is inevitable when performance measures or objectives are not properly aligned with those of others, and will be exacerbated when employees stretch to achieve their personal objectives.

This typically happens with sales people. They are well rewarded on the grounds that they are the ones who generate the business and "without them there would be no business", and commission structures are generally drawn up to reflect both this and the risk they take for choosing this form of remuneration. Yet this very psychology means that they can be more interested in the "chase for business" than the quality of the product or service they are providing. Consequently there is often organisational conflict between the sales force and those left to deliver and administer to customers who had a different perception of what they were going to get from what they actually received. This problem is endemic in the insurance and financial services industry, as well as software sales and consulting, to name just two.

Greed

While improperly aligned incentives will almost invariably cause conflict there is perhaps another cause of potential conflict that warrants identifying in its own right, and that is greed. One can cite the "Enron Syndrome" as a pointer to this, but the issue here is not so much the effectiveness or otherwise of the incentive schemes themselves, but rather the socio-political implications of the incentives paid to executive management. The scale of some of the distributions – particularly when overall corporate performance is far from stellar – not only reinforces some of the points already made about the assessment of performance measurement, but are seen in some quarters to be excessive.

We discussed earlier the disparity between executive and others' pay, but nevertheless there are almost daily newspaper reports of fresh examples which continue to convey the perception of greed on the parts of "the captains of industry". While there are promising signs that investors and shareholders themselves are beginning to revolt against such blatant self-serving on the part of business leaders, there is little evidence of any understanding by the leaders themselves of the fact that this disparity is effectively eroding potential organisational performance. For instance, how do you ensure desired levels of customer service from employees who are explicitly or implicitly treated as second class members of the team?

Yet, there are a number of other points that need to be made here. For instance, "The Times" of 9th October 2002 reported that the three executive directors of Marconi would be in line for bonuses totalling £2 million, or nearly one-and-a-half times their annual salaries, if they were to pull off a rescue of the troubled group. All were board members when the company navigated into the situation from which it needed rescuing! When thousands of employees lost their livelihoods and investors their shirts, this certainly adds insult to injury, and undermines team building.

While not the case in this instance, it is not unknown, when situations turn sour, for executives to exacerbate matters in order to benefit more from the turnaround that follows the subsequent restructuring.

Another more recent example of this would appear to be the situation at Rover, where the jury is still out about the way the company was managed and the extent to which the executive management is alleged to have looked to their own interests first, at the expense of everyone else.

Such scenarios beg the question as to whether common sense comes into play at all with executive remuneration and incentives. The aftermath of the Enron affair and others, and the questions asked about the investment banking industry and their methods, clearly indicate not only that ethics need to be examined more closely, but also that the whole subject of executive incentives and share options needs to be re-evaluated.

WHOSE BUSINESS IS IT?

This is a crucial question that is being asked much more frequently. Many have pointed out that "short-termism" is becoming increasingly endemic in modern commerce and is the natural consequence of the interconnection of:

- The increased emphasis on quarterly results – this is being done on the grounds that "the market" needs to know what is going on and to keep abreast of shifts in patterns.

- The payment of incentives in the form of share options.

- The dilution of share-holdings to the extent that fund managers – who are naturally and inevitably more interested in share price performance and dividends than the long term governance of operations – have become the largest block of shareholders.

- Greater than ever management focus on maximising shareholder value – almost invariably measured by the share price.

- The average age of CEOs who, as Gary Hamel points out in his book "Leading the Revolution", are generally close to retirement and therefore less concerned about the long-term consequences of their decisions than they might otherwise be.

Cynics might suggest that the management focus on shareholder value coincides with the spread of share-option schemes. While it would certainly be interesting to research whether there is any link, the issue here is more to do with consequences than causes. The fact remains that these elements are all increasingly combining to undermine the confidence we can place in the capitalist system.

SHAREHOLDER BENEFITS

The traditional capitalist perspective that the shareholder is the person taking the risk and therefore is entitled to the associated rewards has become so ingrained in capitalist thinking that it is no longer challenged, and anyone who does is seen as "anti-capitalist" - threatening the whole engine of wealth creation that has undisputedly been the most successful system yet devised for raising human living standards.

There is no doubt that this view was justified when capital was scarce and investment, once made, was "locked in" to the business. Yet, nowadays, investment sources are far more diverse and the opportunities and conditions attached generally make it far easier for investors to safeguard their investments.

The size of the market and the ease with which investments can be bought and sold have all combined to reduce the risks, both for individual and corporate investors. This has contributed to a readiness by investors to "churn" their investments wherever they see the possibility of an improved return, which in turn has largely eliminated the traditional investor who not only invested in a business for its own sake, but also constantly monitored the business and its running.

Given the pre-occupation of such shareholders with the market value of the shares rather than the general operations of the business, together with the ease with which they can divest, it is at least debatable whether they are entitled to benefits and rewards on the same historical basis.

MARKET VALUE

Ultimately market value is as much about perception as empirical formula. This has two serious implications. Firstly, the need to find and publish good news becomes paramount. In a climate where the focus is increasingly short term, this increases the pressure to hide any "bad news" and to jump on the treadmill of "continuous growth", whereby business is expected to keep growing, period after period, year after year.

One of the worst aspects of this drive is that it becomes a fixation. No allowances are permitted for changing economic circumstances, while the fundamental economic law of diminishing returns is also completely disregarded. It is basic common sense that, as the base grows, so it becomes increasingly difficult to maintain a consistent pattern of growth. Despite this, targets are set which gradually become impossible. Consequently, each period's results take on disproportionate significance and become a goal in their own right, with continuity and forward thinking almost completely disregarded as rules are bent, and – in a never-ending chain of perpetual deferment – each subsequent period is left to redress the distortions of the last. Inevitably the bubble has to burst and – as debacles like Enron, WorldCom and Parmalat clearly illustrate – the consequences are severe.

Secondly, perceptions are relatively easy to manipulate. Were they not, perhaps management would not be quite so worried about bad news and more confident of their own ability to "ride it out" rather than trying to suppress it or cover it up in the ways just described. One only has to look at how market analysts misrepresented their findings and opinions on WorldCom and Enron, to see the extent to which the whole market is effectively governed by the opinions of a very small group, and how susceptible it is to distortion and manipulation. It may be argued that these are not good examples because they were the result of outright fraud, but rather than mitigating the case, that reinforces it. Not only were the system checks and balances inadequate, but they were able to be circumvented.

Thus, if management is focused on the maximisation of shareholder value and the most powerful shareholders are fund managers who are in turn governed by the returns generated and the freedom of transfer from one fund to another, it is inevitable that the short-term perspective will dominate the long-term. The ultimate effect of this is clearly to kill the goose that lays the golden egg.

It is thus hardly surprising that questions are being asked as to who really has the long-term interests of the business at heart and how those long-term interests can be best addressed.

THE ROLE OF THE EMPLOYEE

The answer has to be the employees. The case has already been made that employees (including management) ultimately determine the level of effectiveness of an organisation, but they also provide the continuity of the day-to-day operations. Although employment is by no means the long-term commitment that it was historically, the fact remains that, as long as they are employed by an organisation, employees collectively are the only stakeholders – apart from the suppliers and arguably the customers – who have a real, ongoing stake in the long-term survival of the business. Even in a buoyant employment market this is the case because:

- The employment association provides an ongoing channel for them to use and develop their talents and abilities, which (arguably) gives some direction and purpose to their lives.

- The current association, regardless of its frustrations and limitations, provides a milestone in the working life of the employee and thus helps to shape future personal circumstances. The employee's future marketability depends not only on the manner in which they carry out their personal responsibilities, but on the ultimate success and survival of the organisation as testimony to their endeavours.

- Future income, in the shape of a pension, may well be affected by the organisation's long-term performance.

Thus, a way has to be found to give employees greater recognition and more power to safeguard the long-term interests of the organisation, and to counter-balance the short-term view that we have seen is often taken by their executive colleagues.

There is a delicious irony in this because it brings us back to the traditional debate about the rights of workers and thence to the whole capitalism versus socialism question. Clearly, however, a fresh slant has to be brought to the table if progress is to be made and the historical conflicts are not to flare up again, with their futile self-righteousness and stagnation-inducing intransigence.

THE SOLUTION

Incentive based remuneration implicitly contradicts traditional economic theory that profit is the return on capital after all other costs, including labour, have been settled. By suggesting that greater profit potential is possible if labour is encouraged to work harder, it supports the case that employees are a major factor in profitability. So maximisation of profits must be a factor of both human and capital investment and both need to be recognised. If greater profits are attainable through incentive remuneration, even greater profits must be possible if the inefficiencies we have just explored can be overcome.

REWARD EFFORT

I believe that this can be achieved by a "labour dividend". This would recognise that profit is not just the reward of financial capital, but also the direct consequence of the human endeavour expended and thus enable profits to be shared between the financial investors and the human investors who have contributed their time, labour and intelligence towards the ongoing success of operations. The creation of a labour dividend would:

1. Through the allocation of a discrete portion of the profits, create a single pool to be shared amongst all employees in the organisation.

2. Facilitate greater teamwork in the organisation by:

- Encouraging each and every employee to focus on optimising organisational efficiency and thereby enhance both the long-term and short-term capabilities of the organisation.

- Eliminating the self-interest and conflict caused by existing personal incentives.

- Encouraging greater co-operation by all to foster the efforts and success of their colleagues.

This may immediately evoke a response that this is simply profit-sharing in another guise, and therefore subject to all the same shortcomings. However, while the principles are broadly the same, this concept goes further by:

- Formalising the extent to which human endeavour is recognised.

- Removing any discretion in the amount attributable and the manner of distribution.

- Eliminating the subjectivity inherent in normal incentive remuneration.
- Creating a more equitable structure that eliminates disparity and most of the potential for conflict.
- Providing a platform like no other for truly effective team working.

More than that, though, it is also the most appropriate basis for creating an environment that encourages self-development with organisational alignment.

FUNDING THE REWARD

This labour dividend would obviously constitute a partial distribution of the profits and thus encounter objections from traditional capitalists who would see it as reducing the returns on equity. To some extent, however, it would be funded by:

- Additional profits gained through more collaborative efforts of employees.
- The saving and reallocation of amounts currently paid as incentive remuneration.

BASIS OF REMUNERATION

The two biggest obstacles to such a concept are:

1. How to distinguish between the financial capital profits and the human capital profits.
2. The thorny issue of how such funds could be equitably shared amongst employees.

DISTINGUISHING FINANCIAL AND HUMAN CAPITAL PROFITS

The method of doing this will necessarily vary from company to company depending upon either or both:

- The stage of the company in its development.
- Whether the business is capital or labour intensive.

For instance, in an industry where there has to be significant financial investment up front with a high degree of risk attached (e.g. 3rd generation mobile phones) it may be reasonable to increase the proportion of profit attributable to the financial capital. Some provision, however, should be made to change the ratio over time as the industry matures and the "venture capitalists" have earned their due reward. In a service industry like tourism it may be more appropriate to have the larger share of profit attributable to human endeavour. Generally, however, I would suggest that basically the profits be split 50-50 between financial reward and human reward.

A more formal way of determining the split would, of course be to divide the share capital into 2 different classes, with Class A shares representing the traditional investment shares and Class B "employee" shares – the "labour" investment. Profit could then be split according to the number of shares of each class in circulation. This would institutionalise the way the Class B shares were issued which would drastically increase the complexity of the scheme, but could also provide the flexibility to accommodate changing circumstances over time.

DISTRIBUTING THE "LABOUR DIVIDEND"

The equitable distribution of labour profits will always be a fundamental issue, critical to the success or otherwise of the scheme. Even where there is formal division of capital into "investment" and "labour" shares along the lines suggested to determine the split between financial and labour profits, there will be considerable debate as to how the shares should be allocated. And, regardless of whether there are formal "labour shares" or not, if the labour dividend is not considered to be distributed equitably, most of the intended benefits of such an arrangement will be lost.

The whole subject is clearly fraught with pitfalls and thus the more simple the scheme the better. Personally, I would favour an arrangement where labour shares, real or notional, are assigned to employees (immediately, or once new employees have completed their initial probationary period) in bands, with the number of shares in each band fixed according to the employee's grade. Dividends on the attributable portion of profits would then be paid in the normal way on a per share basis, with the individual earnings depending on the number of shares held. I would strongly recommend that there be as few bands as possible, to:

- Reflect the growing trend for flatter (less hierarchical) or network organisation structures.
- Minimise the amount of political jostling for promotion in order to justify larger holdings.
- Emphasise the importance of teamwork and recognise the fact that everybody contributes to profit and that contributions and ideas come from all levels of the organisation. After all, seniority is already recognised and remunerated through the grading system and related salary, which in any case will determine the band category.

Example

Perfect Employer Ltd. has decided to pay all staff a labour dividend to reward their efforts and encourage greater teamwork. It has decided against creating a separate category of share capital to facilitate this but has passed a resolution stating:

- Salaries would be paid at a level within the top quartile for the industry, determined in accordance with the annual published results of an independent salary survey.
- There will be no share option schemes allowed.
- There will be no incentive remuneration whatsoever, other than the labour dividend.
- The profits to be distributed as the labour dividend would be 50% of the annual audited profits.

The method of distributing the dividend has been left to management, who have decided that it would be on the basis of "notional shares" awarded to all staff as follows:

- Band A: Executive and Senior Management – 600 shares
- Band B: All other management, senior professionals and expert technicians – 500 shares
- Band C: Employee Grades 7 to 10 – 300 shares
- Band D: Employee Grades 3 to 6 – 200 shares
- Band E: Employee Grades 1 and 2 – 100 shares

I believe that such an arrangement will:

- Eradicate the perfidious share option schemes that undoubtedly lie at the root of so many of today's corporate ills.
- Close the gap between strategy conception and implementation – sometimes one of the biggest problems in corporate management. Instead of executives struggling to sell new strategies to lower echelons of the organisation there will be greater communication and co-operation, building greater teamwork.
- Go some way towards closing the disparity between executive and others' remuneration.
- Encourage all employees to take ownership of the business and generate corporate loyalty and a spirit of teamwork and co-operation.
- Reduce the conflict between management and the workforce and head off the impending struggle with trade unions, which will, over the course of time, become an anachronism.

Notwithstanding this, there remains a need to monitor, recognise and reward individual performance (both good and bad!) Even with such schemes it might still be possible for individual endeavour to remain unrewarded, in precisely the same way mine was in the situation I described earlier, and thus care needs to be taken to ensure this never happens.

NON-PROFIT ORGANISATIONS

The most glaring shortcoming of the labour dividend is that, while it is readily applicable in commercial (for profit) organisations, it does not appear readily transferable to public sector or non-profit organisations. Indeed, given that there are no such things as dividends in such organisations, it would appear impossible.

Yet, incentive remuneration is equally as prevalent in the non-profit sector as it is in the commercial sector. Also, while not profit driven, both public sector and non-profit organisations have a similar objective of optimising their operating efficiency, which implies a pressure on keeping employee costs to a minimum. So there must be a way of migrating these principles.

I believe it is possible, and that a labour dividend could be distributed in very much the same way as in for-profit organisations, with the only significant difference being that, rather than being based on profits, it should be calculated according to a certain formula. While there could be any number of possibilities for deriving such a formula, I would suggest the most logical would be to take the increase in the difference between total receipts and operating costs other than staff costs and distributions from one year to the next, and regard that or an agreed portion thereof as the pool making up the labour dividend to be distributed.

In addition to offering all the same benefits of a labour dividend in a for-profit organisation, such a scheme would also encourage more commercial thinking within a nonprofit organisation, as employees would be more motivated to optimise operating efficiency. If there was no increase, there would be no basis for paying a labour dividend. Apart from anything else, this would eliminate one of the great artificial differences between profit and non-profit organisations and provide for greater transferability of skills between the two.

SOME ADDITIONAL POINTS

Organisational failure always has a human cost, both inside and outside the organisation. Invariably, those who suffer most are employees who have little power to change things but who conscientiously and loyally "do their bit" to meet expectations and support the invariably well-intentioned and often even noble mission promulgated and espoused by management. The extent of the shock of collapse may vary depending on their position in the supply chain and/or the hierarchy of the organisation, but the sense of shock and disappointment, and the feeling of having been let down badly, is universal.

This human loss is no less real than the financial loss suffered by the shareholders. Indeed it is arguably greater. The nature of investment is such that – despite the reductions described earlier – there is always some element of risk, and while the consequences of investment losses may be unfortunate in so far as they reduce personal wealth and affect the pensions and future pension earning power of investors, the loss is hardly as severe as employee loss of basic earning capacity, as well the impact this has on their potential pension capability.

While it is the financial capital that enables any business to get started, it is the human capital – the labour, effort and intelligence of the workforce – that builds on that financial capital and establishes the business. The traditional argument that the labourer earns his wage while the profits are the capitalist's reward for taking all the risks is no longer valid. Enron, WorldCom, Parmalat, et al., prove that the real risks are shared equally by the employees, and management theory has to be changed to take this into account.

INTELLIGENCE VERSUS MANPOWER

Throughout history, people have become used to performing specific jobs according to their skills and training. During the agricultural era, it was largely a case of all available resources being utilised to take advantage of the small window available for harvesting. The labour was manual and the reward tied to the physical capability of the labourer. Then, from the start of the industrial era, the requirement has been for a combination of skilled and semiskilled workers, generally trained to do a specific job. Regardless of the level of skills required, the prevailing attitude was that the skills were always replaceable. This resulted in the popular term "manpower" and even today, ignoring the lack of political correctness of the term, whether the word is used or not, the attitude associated with this belittling view of the workforce is still prevalent in most organisations and in most countries.

As we have seen, the Information Age recognises the need for more responsive employees. Terms such as "learning organisations" and "knowledge management" have come into vogue and underscore the importance of people.

Yet, as soon as times get tough, training is the first expense to be foregone and, worse, these "most important assets" are jettisoned to save costs! With knowledge no longer residing exclusively with management, and decision-making having percolated down the organisation, this is clearly inappropriate. It:

- Perpetuates the historical attitude of people as costs.
- Increases the likelihood of the doom loop becoming a factor.
- Undermines organisational teamwork (one cannot help wondering if the much publicised problems at Jarvis with railway track maintenance are not an example of this?).
- Erodes the trust that is essential to organisational teamwork. All this must inevitably increase the ultimate business risk.

This cannot happen if more than lip service is paid to employees, and the labour dividend is a sure way to ensure this.

WORKERS AS A SOURCE OF IDEAS

In a learning organisation, workers can just as easily be a source of new ideas as managers, and ideas should float up through the company just as easily as they drop down. Also, while strategy will always be the primary domain of the executives, it is no longer their sole domain. Not only is the lowest level employee capable of coming up with ideas that could change the corporate direction, but the successful implementation of any strategy is increasingly dependent on the buy-in and co-operation of the entire staff.

Remember the GEC employee quoted in the introduction, who told Jack Welch, "For 25 years you have paid for my hands when you could have had my brain as well – for nothing." This encapsulates the waste of human resource that has been an integral part of employment practice throughout the Industrial Age and which is still widespread today. Hierarchical organisations create strong divisional and departmental boundaries with "silo-thinking". If they are lucky, employees are regarded as specialists in their field, but any attempt to contribute outside of their "field" is regarded with at best suspicion and at worst contempt.

Some more progressive organisations have attempted to address this through "suggestion schemes", but these are often limited because:

- Most people are naturally reticent. Nearly all of us have an innate respect for authority and so think that others (better than us) must have already thought of everything we have.

- The primary motive for suggestions is often to claim the resultant reward. This often results in serial contributors who put forward ideas they have developed in isolation and which have a far narrower scope than otherwise might have been the case. Almost invariably it leads to "ownership" of ideas, which will likely mitigate against their overall success, as others resist them for personal or parochial reasons.

The labour dividend will simultaneously encourage both self-interest and the company interest. Consequently, employees are likely to co-operate far more and to share ideas for improvement much more readily. Divisional boundaries will become less pronounced, while "us versus them" thinking will be replaced by more collaborative effort, with ideas likely to be thought through better and consequently to be more effective.

CORPORATE RESPONSIVENESS AND STRATEGY IMPLEMENTATION

The previous point carries through here too. Not only will employees be able to contribute more directly to corporate strategy if they have good ideas, but the common interests of both staff and managers will almost inevitably lead to improved communication, greater co-operation and improved teamwork. This should not only make it easier to implement new strategies, but make the organisation more responsive to market pressures and changing circumstances. Change management will thus be less of a challenge.

DIVIDENDS VERSUS INVESTMENT

What proportion of the "labour profits" should be used to pay the labour dividend? With the division between "financial" profits and "labour" profits, it seems logical that financial profit should provide the source of funds for capital reinvestment and consequently the labour profits would then be available in their entirety for distribution as the labour dividend. However, it is more complicated than this.

There may be times when this is not possible, simply because of the scale of the investment that is required. There may also be additional labour costs associated with investment, which make it more appropriate to include a portion of the labour profit as part of the investment. With the increasing acceptance of the concept of human capital, there will be a whole new science of recognising and accounting for the human assets and the investment therein which would call for the partial appropriation of the labour profits specifically. This is a whole subject in itself and not something I propose to explore at this juncture. Suffice to say that some thought will have to go into the question of determining the proportion of the labour profit that is paid out in dividends. Basically, the split between dividend and investment is the traditional spend versus save question that is always one of life's more tricky challenges, even on an individual basis, and there is obviously no definitive answer as to how the split between dividends and retentions should be determined. It is to be hoped, however, that the type of alignment of personal interest and organisational well-being that I have been proposing all along would come into play here too.

There is a precedent for this that suggests that it is not just naïve wishful thinking. A report, "John Lewis reaps investment rewards" in "The Times" (Friday March 7, 2003) states: "Turning in four years of declining profits is not a tactic destined to endear a chairman to shareholders. (John Lewis) however, does not have shareholders but partners. Evidence of what a difference that can make came yesterday with the news that the John Lewis Partnership had recorded an increase in its pre-tax profits for the year to January. ... The Partnership is now beginning to reap the rewards for a massive investment programme. But when retailers invest in refurbishing their stores they suffer a double blow. Not only is the money flowing out to pay for the work, but the disruption to trading floors means that less money flows across the counters. Had (John Lewis) had to pander to the short-term attitudes of investors, (they) would surely not have dared to embark on the projects that have been sapping JLP's finances in recent years. ... But across the portfolio, JLP has been investing for the long term and will continue to do so, but now the rewards are showing through. In both its department stores and its supermarkets, JLP is gathering market share. ... JLP's partners, having blessed (the) ambitious plans, are now rewarded with a bonus of an extra five weeks' pay. And they will continue to benefit from a final salary pension scheme, having voted in favour of that, rather than even higher bonus payments."

With clear objectives and goals in mind, this distribute versus reinvest decision ought not to present too great an issue, but some formal means of resolving any dispute should be agreed upon and built into the scheme up-front. This can then be invoked should any dispute arise and consensus not prove possible. It is also recommended that all employees be specifically alerted to the fact that "profits are not guaranteed" and should therefore be regarded as something beyond their normal income, and that their personal financial affairs should be arranged accordingly. This would minimise the risk of personal overcommitment, and of employees getting into situations where their short-term needs distort their values and outlook and thus outweigh what may be best for the organisation.

John Lewis, with its "communistic" approach of having the employees own the company, is clearly an interesting case. Despite its success and the fact that, in what is recognised as not having been an easy year for retailing, it was "clearly outperforming its competitors", it appears to be regarded as a somewhat eccentric organisation following rather old-fashioned values and not fitting in with the capitalist ideal. In fact John Lewis may warrant further investigation as the pioneer for the new model organisation better equipped for 21st century competition.

WORKER RIGHTS AND TRADE UNIONISM

Perhaps best of all, though, is that this scheme promises to eliminate the historical divide between management and labour. The labour dividend radically alters the role of the worker and means that the historical concept of labour as a cost is no longer valid. Consequently, it does bring something new to the table of "left wing/right wing" conflict and annihilates the root cause of the perpetual ideological clash. Instead, it means that both managers and employees can focus on the common objectives and thus better look after the customer's interests, so securing the long-term viability of the business.

In an age of increasing competitive pressure, society as a whole cannot afford the fallout of industrial action, which is increasingly a cutting-off-one's-nose-to-spite-one's-face phenomenon, where the ultimate loser is the business and so no-one wins. The labour dividend – implemented along the lines suggested – will keep a constant ratio between the incentive earnings of all levels within the organisation and thus redress the increasing disparity in earnings that is so much a bone of contention.

ENHANCING THE LONG-TERM PERSPECTIVE

It is feasible that the long-term interests of the organisation could be further addressed in a number of ways, including some sort of link between the labour dividend and pension rights. This is a complex area that certainly requires more knowledgeable input, but I would suggest any one or more of the following as possible scenarios that might be worth considering:

- Deferring the right to payment of a labour dividend for a year or two. This might be a temporary expedient, undertaken with the consent of employees, during exceptional or particularly difficult times.

- Amending the calculation of the dividend pool to the rolling average of the profits over two or three consecutive years. This would help discourage any tendency to maximise earnings in any one year.

- Mandating that a portion of the dividend be set aside as pension contributions.

- Labour "share rights" vesting in employees permanently after they have been employed by the same company for any agreed length of time – more than (say) ten years.

ELIMINATION OF SHARE OPTION SCHEMES

The point has already been made that share option schemes have contributed to the short-term focus of management, as well as resulted in excessive rewards to executives. However, one of the big attractions of share option schemes has been the fact that they have enabled management to disguise the associated costs, and once again it has only been in the wake of the Enron and WorldCom collapses that there has been a united call for proper accounting disclosure of these schemes.

Replacing share options with a labour dividend removes this issue at a single stroke. By eliminating the practice completely, the question of how to properly and accurately account for them becomes redundant.

The cost of the labour dividend is self evident and readily understood and precludes the vagaries of other incentive schemes and the possible non-disclosure of the true costs. Once again this also removes a potential source of industrial grievance – particularly if the basis of allocation is equitable.

AN END TO THE COMMUNISM VERSUS CAPITALISM DEBATE?

One of the biggest differences between communist and capitalist ideologies has been the debate about the exploitation of the workers for the benefit of the few versus the destruction of the incentive to maximise contribution.

Apart from the fact that this may often be a matter of personal inclination and character more than the consequence of any particular ideology, the labour dividend would go a long way towards removing that issue. It provides a mechanism for aligning worker and capitalist interests whilst at the same time ensuring that both parties are ultimately striving for the same goal. Thus, providing there is consensus as to both the determination of the relative share of profit and the method of distribution – and there is no reason why this should present an insurmountable obstacle if the principles outlined earlier are followed – there is no longer any cause for conflict. An issue that has divided the world for well over a century and cost millions of lives can finally be laid to rest!

THE VITAL COG

Before I get totally carried away, let me pause for a moment to justify my enthusiasm and explain why I believe what I am proposing is such a radical breakthrough in the field of organisational development. Prior to this, the ideas discussed have been largely conceptual and academic. They have, hopefully, both explained the forces behind some of the changes taking place in organisational management, and why implementation efforts thus far have not been totally successful. In doing so, they have also hopefully invoked an awareness of the need to do more and provided the stimulus to take action as well as some idea of the type of action that needs to be taken.

The concept of the labour dividend, however, provides the vital cog that links everything together and offers the broad model to translate theory into practice. The labour dividend will single-handedly do more than anything else to bring about the alignment of person and organisation and facilitate organisational teamwork.

By recognising that there are human costs involved in producing and sustaining profit that entail more than the bare bones of a job description and that are not always adequately addressed through simply paying a wage, grounds are provided for a whole new way of looking at profit creation and distribution. It brings structure to previously intuitive attempts to address organisational effectiveness shortcomings through incentive remuneration. It also resolves some, if not all, of the numerous shortcomings and barely acknowledged side affects of these.

By recognising that profit is rooted in people, it will break down the traditional perspective of people as costs and further the transformation of "Human Resources" into "Human Capital" with all the ramifications that concept entails. By creating a sense of ownership, it will radically alter the nature of employment and should help to break down the perceived divide between "work" and "life". This will stimulate personal development whilst simultaneously helping to ensure that this aligns more closely with the organisational needs.

By providing a structured basis of team development, it will encourage co-operation rather than conflict and conflict resolution rather than criticism. This will create a support system whereby problems are identified and addressed, which will continue the cycle of development that ensures people do not fall back down the doom loop.

By ensuring that everyone has a stake in how the organisation fares, it will facilitate a greater strategic alignment than currently exists in most organisations. There will be a clear "line of sight" between the strategy proposed by the executive and those responsible for making it happen. This will work both ways, in so far as those responsible for the strategy will also be appraised of any potential problems in the day-to-day operations. Effectively the labour dividend will change the whole nature of employment.

Notwithstanding this potential to solve so many organisational development issues virtually single-handedly, this new approach to remuneration should not be seen as a panacea that will create Nirvana. There will still be people whose personal development has taken them beyond the organisation's ability to effectively utilise them; but by recognising them as assets and treating them accordingly it should be considerably easier to accommodate their transfer to a "higher league".

Similarly, there may be personality clashes that make it difficult for people to work together whatever the circumstances. The supportive environment and the cooperation and teamwork, however, should facilitate the speedy resolution of such problems and the development of solutions that benefit all concerned.

The concepts propounded here are not intended to imply "jobs for life". Nevertheless, it is hoped that they will revolutionise the nature of employment contracts, whereby organisations will employ people rather than fill job descriptions. Recruitment will be a "360° process" whereby new employees will not be lured into an immediate "doom loop" prospect on the basis of an ability to do a job immediately, but rather chosen for their ability to grow into the job and beyond. Thus recruitment needs will be defined by subordinates, peers and superiors, who would be internal workmates, customers and suppliers, with potential recruits assessed against how they measure up to those requirements. It is envisaged that such a process will minimise the risk of both poor hires and "empire building", as every potential recruit would be entitled to their share of the labour dividend.

On the other side, this would hopefully also help the wholesale reduction of staff when the organisation encounters a setback or there is a downturn in the economy. Downsizing might still be a viable strategic proposition, but it would have to be within the context of a longer-term strategy supported by the majority of staff and handled in an equitable manner – again most likely in a "360° process".

How does this fit?

If you recall, right at the beginning, when I said organisations needed FAT people I said that the T stood for Tendentious. Well, the labour dividend develops that in spades. If you are looking for people to promote the cause of your organisation, making them partners in the results is guaranteed to achieve this, for now work is no longer "just a job"! Instead employees have a vested interest in how the business performs and, as the example of John Lewis demonstrates, they are able to juxtapose their own interests with those of the business. Interesting, too, is the fact that, although John Lewis is not cheaper than its competitors, it continues to retain customer loyalty and hold on to its market share, which would indicate that there are benefits beyond price to the consumer as well.

Others, too, are starting to recognise the principle behind the concept, although few have taken it quite as far as John Lewis. ASDA, for example, with its £15 million set aside from its annual profits to pay to its employees as a bonus, ranks highly in the top 100 companies in Britain to work for.

While fundamentally the same concept, it is not structured and – as far as I know – is ultimately still at the discretion of executive management although, having set the precedent, it would now be extremely difficult to withdraw.

Also, while at the personal level this makes more tendentious people, at the organisational level it also fosters teamwork. While it does not of itself create teamwork, it eliminates the conflict inherent in so many remuneration systems and thus builds an environment in which everyone is – or should be – ultimately pulling in the same direction. Let us now examine whether this is the case.

CHAPTER 8

BEYOND EMPLOYMENT

"A single day is enough to make us a little larger."
Paul Klee, Swiss painter 1879-1940

This statement encapsulates the inescapable outcome in a lean organisation where continuous improvement is the stated goal and everyone should be trying to improve themselves as part and parcel of the process. In the spirit articulated by Oprah Winfrey and quoted earlier, where everyone *"is doing their best at the moment and being put in the best place for the next moment"*, personal growth is as inevitable as self-fulfilment.

We have already seen how this approach generates both personal fulfilment and alignment. As we have seen, the nature of 21st century competition requires a skilled and highly motivated workforce. The failure of workers to anticipate problems before they occur or to take the initiative and respond to abnormal or unforeseen situations could be disastrous for the organisation. In such an environment, holding back knowledge and effort is a scenario that is simply unacceptable as such behaviour can lead to problems.

Of course, this has been recognised and efforts to address the issue have given rise to a number of new management theories and practices, covering such concepts as "The Learning Organisation"; "Continuous Improvement"; "Six Sigma"; "Knowledge Management", and others. All have made enormous contributions to organisational development and the success of those companies that have adopted them (and the consultants who have promoted them!). Yet, I cannot help wondering if they have not somehow missed a trick. One of my basic principles is that nobody sets out with the intention of doing a bad job. Yet industrial sociologists have repeatedly noted that withholding knowledge and effort has been a salient feature of mass production systems. This has been attributed to the mind-numbing monotony of repetitive and unvarying work, but one has to ask whether the problem doesn't go deeper than that. Is it not simply another result of people losing their individuality and identity at work; of being treated as costs rather than assets?

LESSONS FROM THE AUTOMOTIVE INDUSTRY

The automotive industry is an industry that has transformed itself over the past few decades and there are lessons from that industry that need to be applied in other industries too.

FROM CRAFTSMANSHIP TO MASS PRODUCTION

Henry Ford transformed not just the motor industry but manufacturing generally with his introduction of the assembly-line and pioneering of mass production. Prior to that, it would have been impossible to build two identical cars because, even if built to the same blueprint, contractors did not use a standard gauging system and the machine tools of the day could not cut hardened steel.[1] Consequently, skilled fitters, the residue of the old carriage making industry, would take two parts and file them down until they fitted, and continue with such an iterative process until the whole vehicle was complete. Thus, by this time its dimensions could differ significantly from those of the vehicle on the next stand.

The craft production of the day was characterised by:

- A highly skilled work force who had progressed through a system of apprenticeships to the stage where they could hope to run their own machine shops.

- Decentralised organisations centred in one geographical centre.

---

[1] For a more detailed synopsis of the changes that Henry Ford instigated, and how his methods have in turn been improved, read "The Machine that Changed the World" by James P Womack, Daniel T Jones and Daniel Roos. (Harper Perennial, 1991)

- General-purpose machine tools.
- Low production volumes.

Henry Ford started his revolution by insisting that the same gauging system be used for the entire manufacturing process. This was a crucial first step because it enabled the complete and consistent interchangeability of parts and greatly simplified the effort of attaching them to one another. Only once this had been achieved was it possible to start refining the assembly line, which began with having the parts delivered to the work station and, through a series of progressive steps, moved from having a single assembly stand where the whole car was made – often by one single fitter – through to specialisation where each worker moved from vehicle to vehicle to repeatedly perform the same task in the same way. This resulted in the moving assembly line where the worker remained stationary and the work came to him.

The effect of the standardised gauging was never effectively quantified, but the mass production capability introduced by the assembly line is calculated to have delivered a massive 88% reduction in the effort of producing a vehicle. It is no wonder that mass production and the economies of scale that it delivered spread to nearly all forms of manufacture. Mass production was thus characterised by:

- The interchangeability of parts.
- Division of labour where each employee had a specific job and did not get involved in any other work.
- Greater vertical integration, necessitated by the tighter delivery schedules required to prevent costly production delays where any problem impacted on the entire organisation.
- Specialist machines designed to perform one specific task (rather than the multi-purpose machines of the craftwork era).

In this environment, workers were not expected to volunteer information on operating conditions or make suggestions as to how to improve the process. These were the responsibility of the foreman and the industrial engineer, who would make their suggestions to higher levels of management and await their decisions.

SHORTCOMINGS OF MASS PRODUCTION

There are two significant flaws in the mass production system. Firstly the sequential nature of the system means that when problems are encountered the whole system grinds to a halt, impacting not just on those involved at the specific problem point, but on everyone else down the production line. Secondly, the complete disregard for the individual. Workers are expected to do their job, but are easily replaceable with the minimum of training. Consequently, as we saw earlier, there is little incentive for them to develop – either themselves or their capabilities.

These two flaws combine to create a major problem when it comes to product quality, for not only is there a demotivated workforce who are only going through the motions and who have little concern for quality, but there is an innate reluctance to shut down production when problems are encountered, as the associated costs are seen as prohibitive. As a result, quality becomes an add-on rather than being an integral part of the production process.

FROM MASS PRODUCTION TO LEAN PRODUCTION

It is now fashionable, following a period of fawning devotion in which it was seen to have all the answers, to disparage Japanese management techniques. Nevertheless, they have provided some important lessons and have introduced changes as revolutionary as those of Henry Ford's, and it is worthwhile to take a closer look at these.

CHANGING THE PRODUCTION LINE

Taiichi Ohno, Chief Production Engineer for Toyota, who visited Detroit repeatedly after the Second World War, was appalled at the waste that was inherently part of American automobile manufacture. He recognised that the philosophy of keeping the production line running created a practice of "passing on errors" that caused errors to multiply endlessly, and this contributed significantly to the "rework" costs associated with rectifying them after production. As a result, having already grouped workers into teams under team-leaders rather than foremen, and given them the responsibility for housekeeping, minor tool repairs and quality checking, as well as time for collectively suggesting ways things could be improved, he empowered workers at any level to stop the production line if there was a problem they could not fix. The whole team could then work on the problem. This was a significant contrast to the mass production plants where stopping the line was the responsibility of a senior line manager.

As this system developed, the amount of rework fell continuously and the quality of shipped cars improved steadily. Today, in Toyota assembly plants where every worker can stop the line, yields (the number of cars actually produced in relation to the number scheduled) approach 100% and they have practically no rework areas and perform almost no rework. This is a marked contrast to mass production plants that devote 20% of their plant area and 25% of their total hours to rework. Toyota cars continually have the lowest number of defects of any in the world, although the gap is closing as others start implementing Toyota management practices in their day-to-day production processes.

THE SUPPLY CHAIN

These principles have also been applied to the supply chain. Ohno recognised that efforts to keep the production line going inevitably resulted in high inventory costs and the routine production of parts that were later found to be defective. He also saw that expecting suppliers to work to blueprints with no opportunity to contribute to product design and improvement, whilst competing on cost, also did nothing to improve either service or product quality. Consequently, he organised suppliers into functional tiers and assigned different responsibilities to each tier. First tier suppliers became key, as they were simply given a performance specification and responsibility for the product development, design and manufacture of the end product. They had to co-ordinate all the second tier suppliers they needed to ultimately fabricate the product.

Thus, first tier suppliers were encouraged to talk amongst themselves about improving the design process, something which proved to be mutually beneficial as they specialised in one type of component and did not compete. Similarly, second tier suppliers were easy to group into supplier associations as they were manufacturing specialists and not component competitors.

By adopting this approach, Ohno avoided vertically integrating his suppliers into a single, large bureaucracy and simultaneously disintegrating them into completely independent companies with only a marketplace relationship. First tier suppliers comprised both in-house supply operations that were spun off into independent companies, and independent companies in which Toyota retained a fraction of the equity and which, over time, shared substantial cross holdings in one another. As a result, suppliers were independent companies who performed considerable work for other assemblers and became real profit centres rather than the pseudo profit centres of many vertically integrated mass-production firms.

In addition, Ohno developed the "kanban" or the just-in-time flow of parts system whereby parts are only produced to supply the immediate, quantified requirements of the next step. Of course this means that failure at any stage disrupts the entire production system, but Ohno saw this as a strength rather than a weakness, in that it removed all safety nets and focused every member of the vast productive system on anticipating problems before they became serious. Although it took more than 20 years to develop properly, this system has had extraordinary consequences for productivity, product quality and market responsiveness.

PRODUCT DEVELOPMENT AND ENGINEERING

These principles have been further applied to product development and engineering.

The complexity of motor vehicle manufacture demands enormous efforts from large numbers of people with a vast array of different skills. Mass production techniques divided labour amongst many engineers with specialist skills, creating a real problem with production and with efforts to co-ordinate all these skills to best effect. Ohno addressed this by forming teams that combined both process and industrial engineering, with strong leaders who combined the relevant expertise and whose career paths were determined by team playing skills rather than technical expertise. Here, too, this led to dramatic improvements in productivity, quality and responsiveness to consumer demand.

THE DIFFERENCE

While lean production is an evolutionary step that could never have happened without Ford's work to drive mass production, it is not rocket science to see that the major difference between the two systems is the way in which people are treated. Mass production puts the process first and shapes people around the task, whereas lean production shapes the process around the people and the optimisation of their skills in an effective team environment. It also proves the premise that people are an organisation's primary asset.

It further also proves that while a lean organisation will flourish and thrive, one that is "lean and mean" will inevitably wither and fail.

ARE THESE PRINCIPLES TRANSFERABLE?

While Toyota has led the way in the development of lean production, the rest of the industry has not been slow to learn and the principles I have outlined above have been widely adopted throughout the industry. It is only by taking on board these lessons that the motor industry in the US has been able to survive.

Yet, other industries have been slow to learn the lessons and there seems to be a mindset that they are only applicable to the motor industry or, if the wider possibilities are recognised, to manufacturing generally. Other organisations have remained largely unaware of the lesson and their potential to transform business, although they are universal and could be applied in any environment, including service organisations and particularly financial services and civil services.

In fact, I believe that financial services in particular are at the precise point the US motor industry was thirty years ago and, unless they change their attitude and learn quickly, they will miss the boat completely. For instance, the decision of the major UK banks to relocate their call centre operations to India was a classic example of mass-production thinking. This is because it:

- Is inward rather than outward looking and entirely cost driven.

- Takes no account of customer needs or quality of service.

- Takes no account of existing employees.

Dealing with banks and insurance companies as a customer, one constantly gets the impression of demotivated employees who are more concerned about ensuring that they comply with rigid company policy than providing the customer with service and who, like the dispirited production workers cited earlier, are going through the motions, having neither the ability nor the inclination to do anything beyond the bare minimum. For example:

A friend had gone into business as a sole trader and set up a separate business bank account. This entailed complying with a raft of formalities and bureaucratic red tape. A couple of months later, she decided that it would be better to incorporate and operate as a limited company. She duly started taking the necessary steps to do this, including contacting the bank to ask them to change the name of the account, whereupon she was informed that this could not be done, and that she would have to open a new account. This entailed repeating the same formalities as she had completed two months earlier, including reproducing all the appropriate proof of identity and replicating information that the bank already had. When challenging the need for this, she was told that it was a legal requirement. Fair enough, although with current technology one would have thought that the bank could have used their existing records without any need to waste time and cause unnecessary delays. Her patience, however, was sorely tested when the application form was returned – three weeks later – by the bank on the grounds that she had not, as the company director, authorised her own application to be the sole cheque-signatory!! And if that was not enough, she is continuing to receive statements for her sole trader's account even though the business no longer exists. When she telephoned about this she was told that they could do nothing unless she notified them in writing. So she continues to receive statements every month, which she shreds.

This is not an unusual example, and shows clearly that service companies could benefit from adopting lean production principles.

THE CATALYST

As I pointed out in Chapter 1, Ohno's breakthrough ideas at Toyota were to some extent forced on him by the guarantees given to the striking workers that:

- Pay was to be steeply graded by seniority rather than by specific job function and tied to company profitability through bonus payments.
- Employment was for life.

Ohno recognised the implications of this settlement and the consequent need to get the most out of the workforce over a forty-year period from the moment they joined the company until they reached retirement. Consequently, it made sense to continuously enhance workers' skills and to get the benefit of their knowledge and experience, and this is what drove his pioneering achievements.

Since the challenge is effectively the same one that organisations face in the competitive Information Age market, it would seem that Ohno has already given us the solution.

So, how does the labour dividend compare with the remuneration scheme implemented by Toyota?

TOYOTA-STYLE REMUNERATION VS. THE LABOUR DIVIDEND

The Toyota pay deal clearly introduced a formal link between profitability and payment that – if not new – was certainly on a scale and more universal than anything known prior to that. Yet, perhaps the link between profit and payment is the only major similarity with the labour dividend, while it differs in two significant ways.

Toyota Solution	Labour Dividend
Is classified as a bonus	Is definitely not envisaged to be a bonus
Is steeply graded by seniority	Based on employment grade, but sets out to minimise the grading differential

JOBS-FOR-LIFE

This is slightly trickier, because the labour dividend clearly calls for a fresh look at the whole nature of employment. Yet, while there may be an assumption of jobs-for-life as a natural consequence, this is not actually envisaged to be an integral part of the proposal. There are a number of reasons for this:

- Employment for life actually runs counter to the philosophy of maximising self-potential. It seems that there is always a distinct possibility that an employee will reach a level of personal development that takes them beyond the organisation's ability to effectively utilise them. Consequently, if no other way can be found to stimulate their interest and keep them on a personal development cycle that is mutually beneficial to both parties, it is inevitable that they will start to drop back down the doom loop. This is a lose-lose situation that has to be avoided and which requires an alternative to a job-for-life.

- There may be personality clashes that make it difficult for the individuals involved to perform effectively and/or the organisation to accommodate either or both parties. There have to be satisfactory resolutions to such problems that enable all concerned to move on without any feeling of ill-will or rancour.

- Companies, like products, experience life-cycles of their own and they have to be able to respond to the economic demands of the time. Thus, there has to be a point at which a guaranteed employment policy could become a millstone around the neck, certain to lead to disaster. There has to be some sort of "get-out-of-jail-free" card that allows both parties to walk away from the situation with their dignity and goodwill intact.

Rather ironically, jobs-for-life has been significantly discredited following the downturn in the Japanese economy over the past decade or so. These may be some of the reasons why. So the question is, "Is there some sort of compromise that can be achieved which offers the best of both worlds?"

INFORMATION-AGE EMPLOYMENT

The answer has to lie in a new form of employment contract, centred around the concept of employees as assets, and built on the principles of integrity, trust and partnering. This will help ensure that organisations employ people rather than fill job descriptions and that recruitment will be the "360° process" described earlier.

The problem is perhaps rooted in the generally accepted way in which we look at employment. Webster's dictionary defines employ as, "To make use of; to use or to use the services of." It may just be a reflection of our throw-away Western society with its planned obsolescence, but this implicitly conveys a lack of permanence or even expediency. This is perpetuated in the concept of "hiring" people, which also hints at a temporary arrangement, for Webster defines hire in part as, "To procure for temporary use, for a compensation; to grant temporary use of."

Thus, we perhaps need to move away from such etymological roots and start thinking rather about "co-development contracts" or "mutual benefit partnerships". This would create a totally new mindset that would further the awareness of both parties of their respective responsibilities and provide a framework for co-operation, partnership and teamwork that is currently totally lacking. Replacing the term "employees" with colleagues, associates, partners or team members would perpetuate this culture and the recognition of mutual dependence.

On the other side, this would hopefully also help the wholesale reduction of "headcount" when the organisation encounters a setback or there is a downturn in the economy. Downsizing might still be a viable strategic proposition, but it would have to be within the context of a longer-term strategy supported by the majority and handled in an equitable manner – again most likely on a "360° process" – and in accordance with the rights identified in the "mutual benefit partnership".

By recognising people as assets and treating them accordingly it should be considerably easier to accommodate their transfer to a "higher league" should the situation depicted earlier arise, in which the organisation can no longer accommodate them for mutual benefit. This is not unprecedented, and in fact Toyota themselves arrange the transfer of senior managers with no immediate prospects of promotion within the company to senior positions in supplier firms. The reverse should also be true, and employees who fail "to cut the mustard" could be transferred to lower leagues where their capabilities and potential could be better utilised.

Without trying to sound as though we are attempting to create Utopia, it is anticipated that a supportive environment, with the appropriate co-operation and teamwork, should be able to facilitate the speedy resolution of personnel problems and the development of solutions that benefit all concerned. However, the primary contract should as a matter of course include a clause specifying a "route of arbitration" that will allow an independent third party to decide in the event the two principle parties are unable to agree.

Such policies and procedures will inevitably develop the Fully Aligned Team-workers that are required for 21st century success.

CHAPTER 9

CONCLUSION

John Nash, in "A Beautiful Mind", wrote: *"Adam Smith said that the best result comes from everyone in the group doing what's best for himself. Incomplete! Incomplete! Because the best result comes from everyone in the group doing what's best for himself and the group."*

This encapsulates perfectly the essence of my message and lays the foundation for an environment in which the "economies of trust" can play as important a part as the "economies of scale". Yet, what is truly amazing is not the profundity of the statement, but how glaringly obvious it is or should be. Turning to sport once more to provide the analogy – everyone knows that it is not the team with the best players that wins, but the best team. The winning team is the one that has the strongest "team ethic" where everyone puts the good of the team before their own self-interest or their own individual performance.

We have all at some stage in our lives experienced the "prima donna" who is so talented and so aware of it that they make life unpleasant for all the "lesser mortals" with whom they come into contact and thus completely destroy any team spirit. Sports stars are often used by companies and large organisations as motivational speakers, yet ironically very few organisations draw the parallel between success and teamwork. The old cliché that "no man is an island" does not just apply to life but to nearly all forms of success. There is no getting away from the fact that organisations, by definition, are groups of people and consequently the degree of success they achieve is going to depend on their effectiveness as a team and their ability to perpetuate a strong team ethos.

The age of the "self-made" man is to all intents and purposes over, if it ever truly existed. There may still be people with the vision, charisma and energy to rise above the crowd, but even then their ultimate success will depend on their ability to inspire others. Despite the forces I have described that compel a more team-oriented focus, the fact remains that most organisations continue to operate on a largely hierarchical basis with a top-down chain of command. This is not suitable for the Information Age and such organisations are going to have to "adapt or die".

If you doubt that this is really a problem, or if you think I am exaggerating the need for change, let me quote from the Executive Summary of a report published by Robson Rhodes in October 2004 following a survey of 25 UK blue chip companies including 16 of the FTSE 100, entitled "The Silent Scream of the Unloved Customer."

"Mis-servicing is rapidly becoming one of the most critical issues of the decade for UK companies. As they become ever larger and more sophisticated, many companies are losing touch with their core customers and are either over-providing services that customers do not value or under-providing those they really do. Company boards put customers at the fringe rather than the heart of their strategies, while inflexible management have failed to keep up with rapidly changing customer needs and expectations.

"The impact on profits is significant. The 25 leading blue-chip companies covered for this report, on average, estimated that they could increase their annual profits by around 35%, or £5.5bn, if their business strategies were ideally aligned with the needs of their customers. Extrapolate that for the FTSE 100 companies and UK plc is losing out on potential annual profits of some £20bn.

"An array of factors is responsible for mis-servicing: companies are hampered by:

- *cultures and structures that pay little attention to customer needs;*
- *rigid business models;*

- *IT systems that have not delivered; and*
- *business processes that focus largely on costs and efficiencies rather than customers.*

"CEOs are often remote figures and there is rarely a champion on the board to ensure that customers are at the centre of a company's business. Efforts by companies, since the mid-1990s, to make themselves more efficient, such as the increasing use of offshore call centres, switchboard menus, and on-line form filling, have cut costs, but have also alienated customers. This has been coupled with an ever widening gulf of understanding between companies and their customers, as much market research is done to confirm company thinking rather than to provide genuine customer insight. The result: a mis-servicing crisis, with companies often cutting services that customers find valuable and continuing to provide those they don't want."

£20 billion in lost profits just for the FTSE 100! What then is the cost to UK plc or to the wider world? Think back to the diagram in the introduction showing waste of human potential, and then consider what such inefficiency is costing on a global scale. Yet, how can we expect to provide good customer service if we are relying on people who are uninspired, demotivated and unfulfilled? How can you offer good service without organisational alignment and tendentious employees? The ideas outlined in this book not only describe why such change is needed, but also give a blueprint for how to effect the change.

They start with the individual, and recognition of the need for the individual to pursue self-fulfilment, but balanced against the objectives of the organisation, which in itself calls for greater co-operation and teamwork than is presently the case in most organisations. They build on the concept of the "doom loop" which points out that without stimulation performance will inevitably deteriorate over time, irrespective of how capable the individual is. As a result, there is an ongoing need to keep employees on a personal development curve, failing which there are consequences for the organisation that could go beyond just declining productivity. They expound on the concept that profit is the result of human endeavour and the need to move away from the traditional perception of Human Resources as costs, and stress the need to build on Human Capital and treat employees as the assets as which they are so often described. This would go so far as to change the whole accounting treatment for employees, and suggestions are made as to how this could be done.

Most significant of all, however, is the introduction of a "labour dividend" which extends the logic that it is the people who are responsible for creating profit and rewards them accordingly. Suggestions are made as to how this could be done, and in such a way as to foster the teamwork and mutual ownership we have been describing.

This dividend would replace all existing incentive schemes and share options schemes and thereby redress all their innate shortcomings. This, more than anything else, would encourage the organisational teamwork essential for ongoing success, and delivers on Emerson's statement that:

"Trust men and they will be true to you; treat them greatly and they will show themselves great."

There is little if anything that is new in any of these ideas. They simply plead the cause of "empowerment" and collate and justify a number of different threads of organisational development in a way that has not been done before, in order to help make it happen. Interestingly, much of what is suggested conforms with age-old religious teachings that promote self advancement in the subordination of self, and which have largely been forgotten in a world that has become increasingly self-sufficient.

Yet, despite this self-dependence, there has been a void that has not been filled and which likely accounts for the increasing search for greater fulfilment and "spirituality" in the workplace. I would like to think that these ideas go some way to restoring these values, in a simple and fundamental way without labouring the point and making an issue.

In fact I think there is a nice symmetry here, because the self-effacement that forms such an essential part of good teamwork creates a feel-good factor that helps deliver the transcendence that is the very peak of Maslow's Hierarchy. This realises John Ruskin's vision:

"The highest reward for a man's toil is not what he gets for it, but what he becomes by it."

However, it is important that we do not overlook that it is not just the individual employees who benefit from all the principles outlined in this book. The following graph – reproduced from the Sunday Times 100 Best Companies to Work For – illustrates that companies that look after their people outperform the FTSE by anything up to 100% or even more.

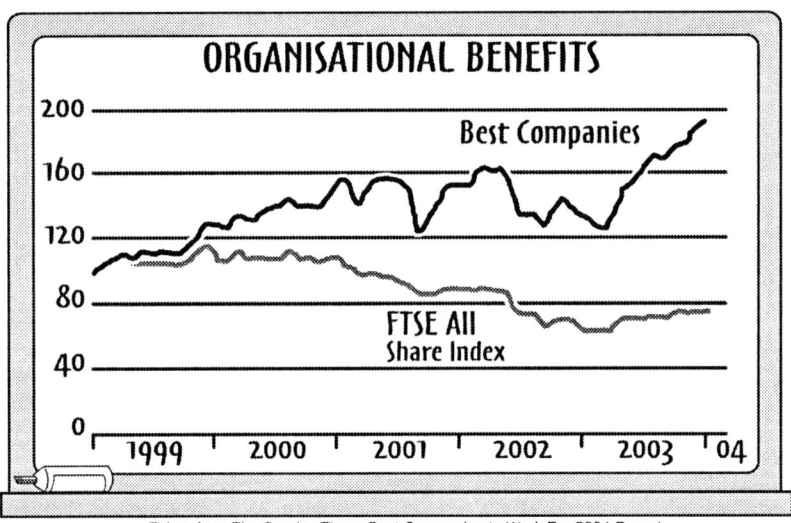

ORGANISATIONAL BENEFITS

Best Companies

FTSE All Share Index

Taken from The Sunday Times Best Companies to Work For 2004 Report

This is hardly surprising because:

- Motivated people will be more productive.

- Motivated people will be more inclined to help one another.

- Problems are more readily identified and resolved by motivated people.

- Organisations that engage motivated people will require fewer of them.

This last point is seminal; a lean organisation by definition is one that minimises its assets – both its human assets and its capital assets. However, if it is to optimise its human capital it has to treat them as assets. If it is "lean and mean" it will continue to look at people as costs and do everything in its power to reduce these, creating insecurity, bitterness and self-interest that undermine organisational efforts. It will have an undernourished workforce; "thin" workers who give the bare minimum, look for any excuse to "take a sickie", leave at the first opportunity to move to greener pastures, and fail to meet either their own expectations or those of the organisation. They thus become a drain on the organisation and the economy as a whole, and economic performance will spiral downwards for all.

On the other hand, an organisation that treats its people as assets and recognises and responds to their individual needs will have FAT workers – people who are Fulfilled, Aware and Tendentious; Fully Aligned Teamworkers – who are committed to ensuring the economic efficiency of which the organisation is truly capable, and will be one which is continually improving as the people better themselves as individuals.

There is no question what kind of organisation people would rather work for. The only question is, what kind of organisation are they working for now?

NOTES

NOTES

Notes

Printed in the United Kingdom
by Lightning Source UK Ltd.
117718UKS00001B/186